D0958973

HISTORY
OF
ARIZONA

By Robert Woznicki Ph.D

OTHER BOOKS BY THE AUTHOR:

1. History of the American-Spanish Military Bases in Spain, 1951-1959

2. History of Western Civilization, co-authored with Dr. Albert Hyma, II Volumes

3. History of Yuma and the Territorial Prison

4. Madame Curie, A Biography

5. Silesian Question

6. Modern History of China

To my parents,
who taught me
love, the work
ethic and traditional
family values.

STATE OF ARIZONA

**ARIZONA COUNTIES
AND
COUNTY SEATS**

TABLE OF CONTENTS

Introduction

My mattress was spread always upon the ground, with a buffalo robe under it and a hair lariat around it, to keep off the snakes; as it is said they do not like to cross them. I found the ground more comfortable than the camp cots which were used by some of the officers, and most of the women. The only Indians we had seen were the peaceful tribes of the Yumas, Cocopahs and Mojaves, who lived along the Colorado. We had not yet entered the land of the dread Apaches.

Martha Summerhayes
from the book
"Vanished Arizona" 1865

Mother nature and man have seldom given to the world in one breath-taking package, such a panoramic view of beauty on this earth, from prehistoric to the modern age, as the State of Arizona.

Arizona's great canyons and sunken deserts, her bold buttes and strange eroded rocks, her painted sands and petrified forests are nature's masterpieces. They are a record of the world's creation.

Only yesterday cowboys with colts and lariats rode their horses down these streets where today automobiles roll. Before that, cliff men, fighting with spears, peopled these mountains and deserts. This is a land where snow lingers in the mountains while the valleys are fragrant with orange and grapefruit blossoms. This is a land where the ever present cactus is in the desert. It is a land of open spaces and dust storms.

New frontiers have always been new horizons of hope. Arizona very well fits this description. It has always been a new frontier and for thousands of people who have gone to Arizona and many who still come, it is a land of hope, of new adventure, of a different style of life.

The name Arizona brings to mind extremes and paradoxes in both geography and climate. Just as Arizona's geography is grand and diverse, so is her history. The record of man in Arizona offers the historian a subject matter of dimension and significance, equal to that of a sovereign nation. As one great historian wrote of Arizona, no other American State would, if isolated, be so truly a great and manificent nation in itself.

Arizona's development has been influenced by all manner of people — explorers, Indians, Padres, trappers, traders, whalers, miners, cattlemen, cowboys, politicians and farmers. A history of Arizona must first do justice to her Indian beginnings and then to the long years of Spanish and Mexican jurisdiction which contributed so much to the shaping of her past and present. It must describe and analyze the main changes brought by Arizona's American era, changes that become increasingly dramatic in the twentieth century.

Arizona and its surrounding territory has always had a reputation as a place of drama in pioneer days. It was a sort of frontier beyond the frontier. In the summer it was God's forsaken place. This was the American Sahara and except for the Northern part of the State, where it was cooler, few cared to live here. It called for a special vocation to live in such a torrid area. In its early history few came to Arizona and very few stayed.

There were really no trees, no grass, no shrubs in many parts of the State. In much of the area there was only the monotonous sands of the desert and the ever present sun. There were always the deadly windstorms of the desert which threatened to cover the hovels of the tiny village with dunes. Plants of the desert were green only immediately after rains, which were few and far between.

In this wasteland then years ago, death was ever present. It was arid and desolate. Many died from lack of water on various journeys to and from Arizona. The curse of the Grim Reaper was always behind you. Deadly snakes, the Gila Monsters, tarantulas, etc., all took their toll.

But the winters in Arizona are the most delightful in America. Only Egypt has a comparable climate. Arizona is a wonderful place for the old and the young in the winter seasons.

The question could be asked, and it is an academic one: Why should anyone want to come and live in Arizona in the old days? The answer can be given by saying that these pathfinders had what we call the PIONEER SPIRIT. This was the passion that made America and it made her great. Such were the pioneers who with great courage settled Arizona and made it the fabulous State that it is.

Today our nation faces an energy crisis. While the expansion of energy usage in Arizona is sharply higher than it is in the nation, the state's consumption on a per capita basis is sixteen percent lower than the national average. The lower per capita usage in Arizona is the result principally of the mild climate of the desert where most of the state's population lives, resulting in large savings in heating fuels. The state does have large deposits of high, volatile, bituminous C rank coal. Numerous sites for new hydro-electric plants also are available. Electric power generating capacity is very adequate today, and large increases in coal-fired and nuclear generating facilities are under construction. Pipelines connect the State to oil refineries in Texas and California. The declining availability of natural gas appears to be the most serious immediate energy problem confronting Arizona today.

Arizona has come a long way since the time when in 1864, J. Ross Browne wrote about Arizona in his "ADVENTURE IN THE APACHE COUNTRY":

"No country that I have yet visited presents as many striking anomalies as Arizona. With millions of acres of the finest arable lands, there was not at the time of our visit, a single farm under cultivation in the Territory; with the richest gold and silver mines, paper money is the common currency, with forts innumerable, there is scarcely any protection to life and property; with extensive pastures, there is little or no stock; with the finest roads, traveling is beset with difficulties, with rivers through every valley, a stranger may die of thirst...... In January one enjoys the luxury of a bath as under a tropical sun, and sleeps under double blankets at night. There are towns without inhabitants, and deserts extensively populated; vegetation where there is no soil, and soil where there is no vegetation. Snow is seen where it is never seen to fall, and ice forms where it never snows. There are Indians who are the most docile in North America, yet travelers are murdered daily by Indians, the most barbarous on earth. The Mexicans have driven the Papagoes from their southern homes, and now seek protection from the Apaches in the Papago villages...... Mines without miners and forts without soldiers are common. Politicians without policy, traders without trade, store-keepers without stores, teamsters without teams, and all without means, form the mass of the white population."

CHAPTER 1.

Some Interesting Facts About Arizona

An embarrassing oversight delayed the opening of the forerunner of Arizona State University at Tempe. It seems that in the rush to construct someone forgot to erect outhouses for the students and faculty. The error was discovered just two days prior to the opening of school and a special meeting was called to remedy the situation. A committee of one board member, Charles Trumbull Hayden, saw to it that the proper facilities were added and the first term in 1866 opened on schedule.

Marshall Trimble
from his book, "Arizona"

1. One of the oldest cities in the United States is the small village of Oraibi, Arizona. It is located in Navajo County near the city of Winslow, Arizona. It is believed to have been in existence since the 14th century. Once the largest of the Hopi towns, its population of 800 at the turn of the century was reduced in 1907, to about half when many of the people left, to found the village of Hotevilla, seven miles west.

2. As early as 1886 women teachers in the school system of Tempe, Arizona, had to abide by these rules:
   1. No smoking or use of spirits.
   2. Marriage or other unseemly behavior was not to be tolerated.
   3. Joining of any Feminist Movement such as the Suffragettes, was forbidden.

As late as 1915, the women teachers found their lot almost as bad with these rules:
   1. Women may not dye their hair.
   2. Two petticoats must be worn.
   3. You are not to keep company with men.
   4. You may not loiter downtown in ice cream stores.
   5. Dresses must be two inches above the ankle.
   6. You may not dress in bright colors.

3. Whoever heard of Arizona having a Navy? Well it did. In 1934 California utility companies were battling Arizona for water rights to the Colorado River. Governor Moeur of Arizona at that time sent two patrol boats, the Julia B and the

Nellie T, to cruise the Colorado River to make sure that all would be aware that Arizona was determined to protect her rights. As it turned out, the two boats, members of the national guard, got tangled in weeds and cable, and had to be towed by their adversaries. Arizona's Navy was disgraced.

4. Arizona has been known for its cowboys and its cactus. But no one would identify Arizona with the ostrich. Yet into Phoenix it came around the year 1885. Women demanded it for their hats and it became a flourishing business in the Valley of the Sun for quite sometime. They required less water than cattle. And they were profitable. The industry lasted to about 1916 when women decided that ostrich feathers were no longer in style.

5. Arizona has the largest nuclear plant in the United States. The Palo Verde Nuclear plant is located about 55 miles west of Phoenix. The plant has three large units. The domed structure that houses the reactor contains 7100 tons of steel rods and 40,000 cubic yards of cement. The cost was about 6 billion dollars. Investing in the project are the Arizona Public Service, Salt River Project, and utilities in California, New Mexico and Texas.

6. On July 3, 1887, the first train rolled into Phoenix, Arizona. The Maricopa and Phoenix Railroad Company offered the town only a branch line that connected via Tempe, with the mail line of the Southern Pacific Railroad at Maricopa. Phoenix had about 3,000 people at that time. Besides some private investors, Maricopa County, as authorized by the territorial legislature, subsidized the line to the tune of 200,000 dollars.

7. The first American mining boom in Arizona was in the Tubac area. Silver mines were developed there by Mexican laborers working for Sylvester Mowry and Charles Poston, the "Father of Arizona," and other well known pioneer entrepreneurs.

8. In 1877 several Mormon families from Utah settled at Lehi, east of Phoenix. The next year another Mormon group started the farming community of Mesa. The Mormon pioneers had been moving into Northern Arizona since the history of Arizona. Today, about 250,000 Mormons live in Arizona.

9. The first man to hold Cabinet rank from Arizona was Stewart L. Udall. He was Secretary of the Interior under President John F. Kennedy. Arizona has lawyers who have been appointed to the Supreme Court, Chief Justice William

Rehnquist and Sandra O'Conner, who is the first woman in our nation to hold this office. Both are considered to hold very conservative ideology.

10. Many historians speculate as to where the word, Arizona, came from. Most say that it came from two Spanish words: Ari (da) zona. Many others say it takes its name from a small settlement on a rough road near the border called in 1730, La Real de Arizona.

11. Near the southern border of the State, Arizona has a preserve of cactus that cannot be found any place in the United States. It is called the Organ Pipe Cactus National Monument. It is an unspoiled desert wilderness, where 330,000 acres flourish, mostly filled with sundry kinds of cacti.

12. During the Second World War, two Japanese-American relocation camps were situated in Arizona. One was at Poston and the other was at the Gila River Indian Reservation. These were Japanese-Americans being placed in camps by orders signed by President Franklin Delano Roosevelt in 1942. Most of the Japanese were from the West Coast area.

13. Green Valley Arizona, is a very well, known retired community located about half way between Nogales and Tucson. Founded in 1964, it is a successful, modern city of about 20,000 residents. One must be at least 55 years of age to buy a residence.

14. There is a Strawberry, Arizona. It is a small community about 110 miles northeast of Phoenix, and it has an elevation of 6,047 feet.

15. Arizona is famous for its major league baseball teams who come here in the spring before the official, major league season begins. Known as the Cactus league, such teams as the Chicago Cubs, Oakland Athletics, San Francisco Giants, the San Diego Padres, the California Angels, Seattle Mariners, the Colorado Rockies and the Milwaukee Brewers attract thousands of baseball fans.

16. In 1864 Charles Debrille Poston, the first Indian Superintendent for Arizona, selected the area known today as the Colorado River Indian Reservation. The reservation was established on March 3, 1865. The reservation is alive with historic and prehistoric archeaological wonders. A mastodon skull estimated to be forty thousand years old, was recently discovered on the reservation.

17. Arizona's most famous Indian trading post is located at Ganado, Arizona. Hubbell's Trading Post is still operating as it has been for nearly a century. It has been designated a National Historic Site.

18. Located adjacent to the tribal administration building of the Kaibab Paiute Indian Reservation in Northern Arizona, is the famous Pipe Springs National Monument. It was established in 1932, to preserve the outstanding works of the early Mormon Pioneers.

19. Perhaps one of the richest reservations in the United States is the Salt River Indian Reservation. It is located in eastern Maricopa County immediately adjacent to Scottsdale, Mesa, and the metropolitan area of Phoenix. The 49,000 acre reservation was created by an Executive Order of June 14, 1879, for the Pima and Maricopa Indian tribes who have inhabited the area for centuries. Scottsdale Community College is located on leased reservation land.

20. The Salt River Canyon often referred to as the mini-Grand Canyon, is a chasm through five hundred million years of geological history, easily viewed along U. S. Highway 60 which follows and crosses the canyon.

21. The celebrated Superstition Mountains are located about forty miles east of Arizona State University. Many people are still challenged by the thought of discovering the "Lost Mine" and search the mountains for its location. The name of the mountains of which Superstition Peak at 5,057 feet is the highest, can be attributed to the legends of the nearby Pima Indians.

22. Mining in Arizona is not confined to gold, silver, and copper. From 1900 to 1945 there was commercial production of mercury from the schists near Sunflower. The remains of these mines are visible from the Beeline Highway to Payson. The Iron King Mine near Humboldt, recently abandoned, was for many years a major producer of lead zinc.

23. Franciscan records of July 4, 1776, tell of explorer's supplies being left at Yuma Indian village of Salvadore Palma. The explorers were packing much of what today's picnickers choose: beans, beef, cheese, biscuits, ham and chocolate.

24. In 1870, seven Sisters of St. Joseph of Carondelet braved dust, Indian attacks, and proposals from woman-hungry men, to establish the Sisters' Convent and Academy for females in Tucson.

25. Arizona has many outstanding people of Polish extraction who have made their talents known in Arizona. Among them are Frank Gordon, Chief Justice of the State Supreme court, Frank Kush, head football coach at Arizona State University, James Ernest, the noted trumpeter of the Big Band era, Dr. Ted Zakrzewski, the well known cardiologist, and Dr. Robert Woznicki Jr., a noted psychiatrist.

26. The extreme Northeast corner of Arizona marks the only place in the United States where four states meet. The Four Corners as they are known are made up of the following states: Utah, Colorado, New Mexico and Arizona.

27. Sylvester Herrera was the state's only winner of the Congressional Medal of Honor in World War II. Fred Ferguson, United States Army helicopter pilot, won the Congressional Medal of Honor in the Vietnam War.

28. The summers in Yuma are known for their intense heat. The summer thermometer often hovers near 120 degrees. The story is told of the reckless sinner who passed on and went down to his unfortunate reward. When he got there, he sent back for his blankets. It was cooler there than in Yuma.

29. Ice was first manufactured in Phoenix in 1879. In 1880 the medical service industry was initiated in Arizona with the building of St. Mary's Hospital in Tucson, the only hospital in the state at that time. The first public rodeo in the United States was held in Prescott in 1888. The first telephone system was established in Phoenix in 1892 by the Sunset Telephone and Telegraph Company.

30. One of Arizona's best-known characteristics is that it is a state mostly owned or managed by the federal government. Of its 114,000 square miles, only 15 percent (17,000 miles) is in private hands. The remainder is made up of federal forests, wilderness, parks, Indian reservations and military installations. It is quite obvious then, that Arizona has a very small tax base. Also that its politicians for years have been battling the Federal Government, which tries to dominate policy in this state.

CHAPTER 2.

Symbols of Arizona

"Arizona is blessed with a panoramic beauty that almost defies description. Only a limited number of poets, painters, and photographers have been able to do justice to her splendor."

Marshall Trimble

Arizona stretches north to south about four hundred miles while the east to west width is about three hundred, thirty-five miles. Altogether Arizona contains 113,956 square miles, of which about 145 are water. Arizona is the nation's sixth largest state in area. The northern part of the State is a land of high mountains and plateaus streaked by deep, penetrating canyons and snow in the winter season. Near Flagstaff, Arizona, Humphreys Peak, tops all elevations at 12,670 feet high. In the high plateau region is the fabulous Grand Canyon, one of the seven wonders of the world. It has an average vertical depth of one mile. One cannot really describe the pure and awesome beauty of this region. About 2½ million people now live in Arizona.

The southern part of the State centers around the well known cities of Tucson and Phoenix. Most people know these areas for their heat and cactus. This is desert country and when one travels to the city of Yuma, one knows what the Sahara must be like in the summertime. But the glorious winter weather of these celebrated resort towns has made Arizona famous. Yet even in this land of the coyote and the gila monster, everthing is not the same arid type of topography. An hour's drive out of Tucson, for example, will take you from saguaro-like desert to cool forests atop the famous Mount Lemmon. Truly Arizona is a state of amazing variations of climate and topography.

We have learned from archeological studies at the Ventana Cave, northwest of Tucson, that living humans were in the Arizona area some 20,000 years ago. We have learned from the studies of various Indian tribes as well as excavations at Casa Grande, Tuzigoot and Kinishba, that Arizona indeed had early residents going years and years into the past.

Arizona has a number of symbols of Statehood. Let us begin with the state flag.

The State flag represents the copper star of Arizona rising from a blue field in the face of the setting sun. Old gold and blue are the colors of the state. The blue is the same shade as that of the flag of the United States. The lower half of the flag is a blue field. The upper half is divided into thirteen equal segments of rays which start at the center and continue to the edges of the flag, consisting of six yellow and seven red rays. A five-pointed copper star, symbolic of the state's enormous copper industry, is superimposed on the center of the flag.

The state flower is the blossom of the saguaro cactus, the largest cactus found in the United States. The saguaro (sah-war-oh), or Giant Cactus (Carnagia gigantes), is found in Arizona and Northern Mexico with a very few scattered along the Colorado River in California. This cactus grows to a height of fifty feet, and lives to an age of from 150 to 200 years. Its pure, white, waxy flowers appear in garlands on the tips of the long arms of the plant in May and June.

Arizona's state bird, the cactus wren, is a true lover of the desert country. The wren's nests in cactus plants are common. The more thorny plants serve as protection. A woody-brown bird, with a speckled breast, he will build not one, but several nests, using one as a home and the others as decoys from his enemies. Nesting time for the cactus wren begins as early as March and extends into June.

The twenty-first Arizona State Legislature, second regular session, designated the palo verde (genus Cercidium) as Arizona's state tree. The palo verde (from the Spanish meaning "green stick" or green pole) is one of the beautiful trees of the desert. When it blossoms, generally in April or May, depending on elevation, it is a blaze of shimmering, yellow gold. There are two native species of palo verde Cercidium in Arizona, the blue palo verde, characterized by a blue-green color of the branches and leaves; and the foothill palo verde characterized by the yellow-green color of branches and leaves. Both bear a profusion of yellow blossoms when in bloom.

But the greatest symbol is the Grand Canyon. God shed his light on Arizona when he created the Grand Canyon. It is a broad intrically sculptured chasm that contains between its outer walls many colorful peaks, buttes, and canyons. It ranges in width from 4 to 18 miles and in length about 217 miles. The deepest and most impressively beautiful section, 56 miles long, is within Grand Canyon National Park, through which the river winds for 105 miles. At 8,200 feet above sea level, the North rim is 1200 feet higher than the South Rim.

The first sighting of the Grand Canyon is credited to the Coronado expedition of 1540 and subsequent discovery by two Spanish Priests, Francisco Garces and Silvestre de Escalante, in 1776.

Grand Canyon National Park, containing 673,575 acres, was created in 1919. Many pueblo and cliff dweller ruins, with accompanying artifacts, indicate prehistoric occupation. There are about five Indian tribes living on nearby reservations.

Other symbols of a lesser degree would be the Kachina Doll, the cowboys and Indians who played such an important role in the saga of this state, the beauties of the desert, the Arabian horses which are raised here, the fantastic weather which attracts millions of tourists each year, the Indian jewelry that is worn by millions all over the world and the Arizona State University football team which played in the Rose Bowl on January 1, 1987, and defeated the University of Michigan 22 - 15.

Another museum of great interest can be visited by going north on Highway 17 about 25 miles from Phoenix to Pioneer, Arizona. Here is a living history museum of great note recalling the 1870s-1890s of Arizona legends. It is the largest museum west of the Mississippi. Pioneer features buildings moved from original sites from all over Arizona. The furniture is all western and the working personnel all wear western clothes dating back to the 1890s. Many school children are brought there and guided tours teach these youngsters the realities of the golden West of the past.

CHAPTER 3.

Spanish Missions Dominate Arizona History

"Passing very near it, we entered upon the more than forty leagues of coast and new road between there and the mouth of the Rio Grande (Gila) and its confluence with the Rio Colorado. By the natives whom we found along the road, we were received with all love. We spent the 22nd of February, the day of the Chair of St. Peter in Antioch, on the Rio Grande, where more than fifty natives, Pima, Yumas, Opas, and Cocomaricopas, had gathered. We named the pass and rancheria San Pedro and another rancheria lower down was named San Pablo."

Eusebio Francisco Kino S.J.
in Memoirs of Pimeria Alta,
February 7, 1699.

Located in Arizona, the "baby state" of the United States, are Spanish missions surrounded by legends, history and strong religious convictions, all of which have had vital roles in the development of the territory of Arizona.

When the Spaniards first came into Southern Arizona during the seventeenth century to establish the mission of San Xavier, they visited the Indian village of Bac, the site which today is Tucson, oldest and second largest city in the State. The mission was named San Xavier del Bac because of the nearby village.
(See front cover for photo of San Xavier)

The group of Spanish settlers, headed by Father Eusebio Francisco Kino, discovered that most of the villages of the Hohokam culture were in ruins — the dwellings occupied at the time were dome-shaped mud and brush huts, rectangular mud and brush houses or open-sided shelters. Thus, the first work of the Spanish missionaries was to teach the Indians to make adobe brick by churning a mixture of mud and straw with their bare feet, forming blocks by hand and setting them in the sun to bake. The Indians were encouraged to build new homes with their new adobe bricks around the new mission.

Father Kino's Spanish priests also taught the Indians the fundamentals of irrigation and farming. San Xavier's founder recorded that on the grounds of the mission he grew wheat, maize, grapes, figs, oranges and melons — crops which the Papagos continue to raise on their nearby farms. The Spanish are also credited with having been the first to teach the Indians to grind their maize with grinding stones, one of the old fashioned methods still used by Arizona tribes.

San Xavier's church is the only one of the early Spanish churches now in use, the remaining twelve other missions established by Father Kino and his followers had been deserted years ago and left in ruins.

Now a landmark of the tide of the Spanish Conquest, the ruins at Tumacacori, located eighteen miles north of Nogales, have been made a National Monument under the supervision of the National Park Service. The mission was established late in the seventeenth century and like San Xavier was founded by Jesuit Padre Kino. Tumacacori was one of the chain of Catholic missions founded by the Spanish extending from Mexico to California.

The church at the Tumacacori Mission was built by the Indian followers of the Spaniards and was constructed with sun-dried adobe bricks laid in mud mortar. Though generally typical of mission architecture, the rectangular shaped church at Tumacacori with its massive square corner tower and superimposed columns, suggests the earlier and more classic traditions established in Spain by Juan de Herrera. More than fifty feet wide and one hundred feet long, the church has black and red pebbles imbedded in the mortar on the north wall.

Adjacent to the church, forming a hollow square, were priests' residences which show evidence of having been small, comfortable dwellings. Located on the east side of the church was an oblong building where metallurgical operations were carried on. At the present time remains of furnaces and quantities of slag attest the purpose of the building.

The church building at Tumacacori, which today is under the jurisdiction of National Park Service employees, was dedicated in 1822, but abandoned a few years later when the Franciscans were expelled from Mexico shortly after Mexico won her independence from Spain.

At one time the mission formed a respectable village with its church, adjoining buildings, homes and gardens — vines and fruit trees still grow there.

The date of the birth of Father Kino, is not known, but is believed by historians to have been about 1640. Before accepting priestly orders he had acquired a reputation as a mathematician. The reason Father Kino, subsequently known as the Great Apostle to the Pimas, became a priest is said to have been that he believed he had been restored to health from a dangerous illness, through the intervention of St. Francis Xavier and he determined to devote his life to the conversion of the heathen in America. He added Francisco to his name, which became Eusebio Francisco Quino, afterward changed to Kino.

The keeper of a very detailed diary, Father Kino recorded for future generations accounts of his hardships and accomplishments in establishing the Arizona missions. It is through the records passed down by the padre that Arizonans have come to know the history surrounding the founding of the early missions.

Arizona has a large percentage of Indians. The leading tribes are the Pima, the Apaches, the Navajos, the Hopi, the Maricopa, and the Papago. It was for these tribes that the Spanish first built the missions in Arizona. It was they that the early priests converted, and they again were the ones to use the missions as garrisons during their wars — the towers at Tumacacori served as look-outs for the Apaches on numerous occasions. Even now the congregation at San Xavier, the only active mission church, is composed mostly of Papago Indians.

Today the stately white mission buildings at San Xavier and the ruins of the Tumacacori Mission are two of the main attractions in Arizona.

Historians say that thirteen missions and rancherias were at one time established in the territory which today comprise the State of Arizona; however, many of these missions were in existence only a short while, some having closed in 1736 when Father Ignacio Keller visited the territory. One of the early missions, San Miguel de Guevavi, was named for the Indian village, Guevavi, which has disappeared from modern maps. The mission was established by Father Kino and Father Juan Maria de Salvatierra who had a large Indian following. The Sobahpuris Indians, who lived at Guevavi and were responsible for the founding of the mission there, traveled two hundred miles to find the padres and ask them to come to establish their mission. The continuing interest in the Catholic faith by Arizonans is evidenced in the fact, that over fifty percent of the state's population today is Catholic.

Among the earlier missions were Immaculate Conception and St. Andrew, both of which were established by Father Kino. The physical buildings of the missions have not been preserved. Sonoitac, another of the early Arizona missions, was deserted around 1784.

The mission of San Augustin del Tucson was founded in 1769 by Father Garces, a Franciscan monk. Father Garces was a leader in the early mission work and it was he who made Tucson a walled city. He was killed in 1781 by the Indians.

Established in villages forming a chain from Mexico City to the Pacific Coast, the majority of the early missions are today connected by a modern west coast highway popularly known as "El Camino Real."

In general the Arizona missions all followed the same building pattern. The churches, which dominated the grounds of the missions, were rectangular buildings. There were some few exceptions in the mission chain, notably the San Xavier church which was cruciform.

The architecture of the early Spanish fathers, used for their shrines during the seventeenth century, has been handed down through the history of Arizona. Many of the modern schools of the state are in various ways duplicates of the mission buildings. The adobe brick, first made by the Indians under the supervision of the Spaniards, is used for modern Arizona's municipal buildings and homes.

As the Pilgrims were landing at Plymouth Rock in the Eastern United States, the Spanish padres were advancing into the western territory of Arizona and leaving behind them an indelible impression which even today dominates the religion, architecture and customs of Arizona.

When Mexico gained its independence from Spain in 1821, the new government decided to break up the mission system. The congress in Mexico City made all Spanish clergy take an oath of loyalty to the new government. All foreign missionaries were sent back to their homeland. The philosophy of the Mexican government was anti-Spanish. The missions slowly disappeared. In 1834 the Mexican government began to sell the mission lands. In 1844 the mission land near the famous church of Tumacacori, Arizona, was sold at public auction for $500.

CHAPTER 4.

Scenic Wonders

The first missionaries who viewed the Grand Canyon described it as one of God's finest creations. The modern cynic might mutter acidly that it looks like a bad case of soil erosion, while a cowboy might gaze into its vast abyss respectfully and quietly observe that it would be a "hell of a place to lose a cow."

Marshall Trimble
in his book on Arizona

Just southeast of the Grand Canyon National Park lies another of nature's wonders — the Painted Desert.

The Painted Desert extends for three hundred miles along the north band of the Little Colorado River. Eons of rain and wind have exposed the highly-colored shales, marls and sandstones. Warm, almost unreal tints waver across the sands, dance along the mesa tops, stain the lomas and ledges, and splash scarlet hues from horizon to horizon. The caprices of heat, light and desert dust frequently change the colors from blue, amethyst and saffron to russet, lilac and blood red. At times even the air above this lonely land glows with a pink mist or a purple haze. In the early morning and evening the mesas seem to broaden. Mountains a hundred miles away rise in clear profile.

In one of the most colorful sections of the Painted Desert is Dinosaur Canyon. Here, in the canyons and on the cliffs, have been uncovered over three hundred dinosaur tracks, the largest number ever found anywhere in the world. The largest track measures twenty inches in length. The imprints were probably left there at least 40,000,000 years ago. The trip to Dinosaur Canyon in late afternoon when the setting sun sets fire to the red cliffs is one of the memorable occasions in a lifetime.

The Painted Desert was included in 1936 as an addition to the Petrified Forest National Monument — one of Arizona's superb national masterpieces. This National Monument, which covers 90,302 acres, takes in also much territory south of the Painted Desert region and contains altogether six separate forests of petrified wood. This area was a low-lying swamp basin in Triassic time, 160,000,000 years ago and the trees were floated in by streams flowing from the surrounding highlands. The logs were then buried by stream deposits and by volcanic ash. While buried, the wood of the logs was replaced by the mineral silica, or quartz, carried in solution by ground waters. Iron oxide and other minerals stained the silica to form the present rainbow colors. Later the region was uplifted and the action of wind and rain removed the covering sediments to expose the logs.

Of the six forests, Rainbow Forest is the largest and best known. Many of the trunks are more than one hundred feet in length. The outer sections are usually reddish brown, but the cross sections reveal every tint of the rainbow. Some have been reduced by the elements into piles of chipped agate, onyx, carnelian and jasper.

An Indian legend tells of a goddess, hungry, cold, and exhausted, who was pleased when she found hundreds of logs lying on the ground. She killed a rabbit with a club, expecting to cook it. But the logs were too wet to burn. Enraged, she cursed the spot, turning the logs to stone so they could never burn.

In this same broad circle of great natural sights, north of the Petrified Forest National Monument and northwest of the Grand Canyon, lies Monument Valley. This valley is famous for outcrops of red sandstone, several hundred feet high, which have been eroded into pillars and spires or into huge rectangular blocks with grooved sides suggesting columns. (See front cover). From a distance these rose-colored rock monuments, looming above the desert, have the aspect of the ruins of gigantic Greek temples.

Historically this valley is interesting having been at one time the home of the Navajo Indians. When Kit Carson rounded up this tribe in Canyon de Chelly in 1863-64, Chief Hoskinni led his people into this area, where he lived in complete independence till his death in 1909.

Monument Valley has its legend of hidden treasure. In 1880 two men named Merrick and Mitchell made a prospecting trip into the valley and returned with quantities of almost pure silver. From their second trip neither returned. They were found shot. Mitchell Butte and Merrick Butte are the natural monuments to the two men.

We pass over other great natural wonders in Arizona which are chiefly geologic records of past ages. These include: — the natural bridges — among them Rainbow Bridge, so called from

14

its rainbow arch; Sunset Crater, the almost perfectly preserved crater of an extinct volcano; El Morro National Monument, the great buff monolith resembling a fort on the old road followed by the Spanish conquistadores of the seventeenth and early eighteenth centuries and bearing inscriptions of their travels.

We come now to nature's living miracles in the form of the giant cacti in Saguaro National Monument, in the Southwestern part of the state. The Saguaro National Monument, seventeen miles east of Tucson, is a tract of more than 63,000 acres containing a forest of twenty-six species of cacti, the greatest of them, the Saguaro. These corrugated giants with their perpendicular branches look more like the strange dreams of a modern artist than living growths. Many of them are more than one hundred years old and have attained a height of fifty feet. They are a comparatively rare species, as their habitat is limited to Southern Arizona and Northern Mexico. The Saguaro's ability to store water against the dry season is remarkable. Water absorbed during the rainy season is sucked into the trunk, which expands its spine-covered accordion pleats to serve as a reservoir. A mature plant may take up as much as a ton of water following a soaking rain.

In spring the Saguaro bears waxy, white blossoms at the ends of its branches. These develop, in late June, into purple fruit. The fruit is a favorite food of the Papago and Pima Indians — its harvesting is the occasion for a Papago festival. The Indians eat the juicy red pulp, both fresh and sun-dried, and boil the juice into a syrup that is very intoxicating when allowed to ferment. The ripe fruits furnish food, too, for several varieties of birds, particularly the whitewinged dove, and for small mammals such as chipmunks and ground squirrels.

The giant cacti provide nesting sites for many kinds of birds including the gilded flicker, the gila woodpecker and desert wren. Other wild life seen in the Saguaro National Monument include mule deer, wild hogs, coyotes, badgers, rabbits and foxes.

As for other forms of vegetation, in April and May, the desert is yellow with the bloom of the Palo Verde and mesquite trees; while hillsides are aflame with the red flowers of the ocotillo.

Of equal interest with Arizona's magnificent geological spectacles are its archeological sights. The state is covered with the remains of early civilizations. Arizona has been the home of hair aborigines who stoned to death the giant sloth, the mammoth and many other beasts now extinct. It has been the home of nomads who sheltered in natural caves, hunted with spears and bows, yet developed the art of basketry to a high point. Cliff dwellers who built homes of stone and shaped clay into pottery lived here. Likewise pastoral tribes who built pueblos and planted corn and cotton beside irrigation canals left their mark here.

Important among the archeological treasure spots in the Sunset State is the Canyon de Chelly National Monument in Northeastern Arizona, within the Navajo Indian Reservation. This monument covers 83,840 acres and includes Canyon de Chelly and Canyon del Muerto.

The walls of the sandstone canyons rise to heights of 700 to 1,000 feet. In natural crevices in their sides are many cliff-dweller ruins. Perhaps the most famous is the White House Pueblo, which was occupied for 200 years from about 1060 to 1275.

In this one National Monument can be seen the development of ancient Southwestern Civilizations, with but few periods lacking.

More recent history credits the Spanish with having entered the Canyon de Chelly and fought with the Navajos of this region in the early 19th century. Later in 1863-64, it was the scene of Kit Carson's greatest feat when he campaigned all through this canyon and rounded up 7,000 Navajos and exiled them to New Mexico in their final defeat. The difficulties were described in a report of 1864, which said:

"This is the first time any troops have been able to pass through the Canyon de Chelly, which, for its great depth, its length, its perpendicular walls, and its labyrinthine character, has been regarded by eminent geologists as the most remarkable upon the face of the globe. It has been the great fortress of the tribe since time began. To this point they fled when pressed by our troops. Many military commanders have made an attempt to go through it, but had to retrace their steps. It was reserved for Colonel Carson to be the first to succeed."

Along the canyon bottoms, where the water can be utilized for irrigation, about 500 Navajos live.

Montezuma Castle National Monument in the Verde Valley of Central Arizona protects another group of these cliff dwellings, among the best preserved ruins in the Southwest. Montezuma Castle, a five-story, twenty-room structure, is the best of these cliff homes which honey-comb a limestone cliff bordering Beaver Creek. With its foundation nearly 50 feet above the cliff base, the Castle is reached by a series of ladders, and is 40 feet high. It is remarkably well-preserved owning to the fact that it is protected by the overhanging cliff.

Near the Castle are many smaller structures of from one to five rooms. Some three hundred to three hundred fifty persons probably had their homes in these prehistoric apartment houses, which were occupied from the eleventh to the fourteenth centuries.

The sedentary farmers who occupied this fertile valley were driven to take shelter from marauding warlike tribes in their high rock niches. The visitor can picture some keen-eyed sentinel discovering enemies on the far horizon and then warning all the farmers working in the fields below by thumping on a huge tom-tom.

In 1694 the Spanish missionary, Father Eusebio Francisco Kino, discovered a large ruin on the Gila River which he named Casa Grande. At that time the ruins must have been standing in much the same condition that they are today, except that a large cement roof has been built over them to protect them.

The Casa Grande is located in Casa National Monument, 67 miles north of Tucson. It was erected more than 800 years ago as a watch tower by the prehistoric farmers who lived in the six villages which are included in the reservation. It stands four stories in its center room and three stories in its four outside rooms, the walls rising about forty feet above the desert level.

It is believed that the Casa Grande people, called the Hohokam Indians, were originally nomads who came to the Valley about 2,000 years ago. They settled here and developed an irrigation system, the ruins of which are still seen. The Hohokams left records of their civilization, including pottery, finely engraved necklaces, rings, bracelets and bangles of shell.

Other important records of prehistoric man are found at Navajo National Monument, which contains remarkable thirteenth century pueblo cliff dwellings; at Tonto National Monument, which has fourteenth century Pueblo cliff homes. Altogether there are probably 100,000 of these prehistoric ruins in Arizona.

CHAPTER 5.

A Look at History

"Tucson is cursed by the presence of two or three hundred of the most infamous scoundrels it is possible to conceive. Innocent and unoffending men were shot down or bowie-knifed merely for the pleasure of witnessing their death agonies. Men walked the streets with double barreled shotguns, hunting each other as sportsmen hunt for game. In the graveyard there were 47 graves of white men in 1860, and of that number only 2 died natural deaths."

John C. Cremony, 1860,

Many think of Arizona and its past in terms of cowboys fighting Indians. Many young people watching a John Wayne movie or a late TV scenario have the image of Arizona as the wild West. The old and the young just think of Arizona as dusty and full of western towns which have saloons and cowboys — and maybe an honest sheriff or two. The period of the cowboy and Indian lasted only a very short time in Arizona history, 1850-1886. Actually it was a small part of a saga that is rich with people, various cultures, violence and wars, and a panorama of events unparalleled in the development of any of the fifty states.

In 1528 a Spanish explorer named Alvar Cabeze de Vaca landed in what is now Florida with an exploring party. They were attacked by Indians and all were killed but Cabeze de Vaca, two other Spaniards, and a big, black man, called Estevan. The Indians took them captive. Cabeza soon convinced them of his abilities as a medicine man and they allowed him and his followers to go about as they pleased. They were not given their full freedom, however, until one day they met some Conquistadores coming north from Mexico. These were the first Europeans they had seen in years. Cabeza de Vaca was to return with them to Mexico City, where he told all about the seven, fabled cities of gold and his years with the Indians. He had mastered the Indian's language and probably knew more about their culture than

18

any man alive with European blood at that time. He excited all Mexico City about the cities of gold and many wanted to return and look for it in the land of the North, called Pimeria Alta.

The Viceroy of Mexico, Mendoza, now sent Fray Marcos de Niza with some Indian servants, and the black man, Estavan, to seek the gold. Father Marcos sent Estevan and some of the Indians ahead. If the land was good, Estevan was to send back two small sticks in the form of a cross. The better the land, the larger the cross was to be. Imagine Father Marcos' surprise when a short time later two Indians appeared carrying a cross as large as they were. He was delighted and hurried after the Indian guides hoping to catch up with Estevan. When they arrived at the San Pedro River in what is now Arizona, they found some of the camp sites used by Estevan. Sad to say, they were to learn that Estevan had been killed by hostile Indians.

The Indian guides were frightened and did not want to proceed, but Fray Marcos persuaded them to go on for a few more days. Finally, one evening, they could see a "city" in the distance. Perhaps to the Indians a village of some 200 huts seemed large. But one wonders how Fray de Marcos could have been mistaken. And mistaken he was, for he was to report that this was the first of the seven cities of gold. Perhaps the tiny flakes of mica in the adobe walls glinted in the rays of the setting sun, and made the city look like it was golden. After all it was twilight and the human eye does deceive itself at this time of the day. At any rate the loquacious Fray de Marcos returned to Mexico City and told all that he had seen one of the golden cities.

Now the Spaniards prepared to search for the cities in earnest.

Three hundred soldiers led by Francisco Vasquez de Coronado, hundreds of Indian slaves, and several priests made up the new expedition. They had horses, cattle, sheep, hogs, goats, and many pack animals. Their expedition was to cost about two million dollars. They must have been an exciting sight as they started out; the Conquistadores in their silks and fine armor, the long robed priests, the foot soldiers, Indian slaves, pack animals and finally the animals being herded along.

They sent some of their supplies by two ships up the Gulf of California. The ship's captain was named Alarcon. He and his men found the mouth of the Colorado River and sailed north on it until it became too shallow for the ships. He is said to be the first European to see the present site of Yuma, Arizona.

19

Coronado and his men came as far as Northern Arizona but found only small villages. They conquered some of these and took the available food but they found no gold. One of the soldiers found the Hopi villages. The Hopis were a peaceful tribe and soon made friends with the Spaniards. They told them of a large river west of the villages. One Spaniard, Captain Garcia de Cardenas, went to investigate and returned and told Coronado that the river was useless to them as it was at the bottom of a mile deep canyon. He had discovered the famous Grand Canyon on the Colorado River.

Finally, in 1542, after several years of unsuccessful searching, the remnants of the expedition returned to Mexico City, ragged and empty handed. Poor Fray de Marcos was blamed for their failures and he sadly returned to Spain.

Forty years went by, then another Spaniard, Antonio de Espejo and Fray Bernardina Beltran, returned to Arizona and discovered silver in the Prescott area. Others followed and mining began in Central Arizona, but the Indians were hostile and the mines were so far from Mexico that working them was not very profitable.

At last the Spanish Padres, who were Jesuit priests, came and with engineering skills acquired from their advanced culture, began to build a chain of missions which changed the complexion of the West. They brought knowledge of farming and medicine and totally upgraded the life of the Indians. Many converted to Catholicism, for the Jesuits were excellent teachers.

Later in 1768, the Franciscan Fathers, another group of Roman Catholic Priests, made their way into the pages of Arizona history. Fray Francisco Garces came and made San Xavier his headquarters. He wanted to establish a trail between these and the missions in Southern California where another Franciscan, Father Junipero Serra, held a monumental reputation as the Father of the California Missions.

Life in Southern Arizona flourished even though some marauding bands of Indians occasionally raided the mission communities and stole the livestock. There were no huge problems as long as the Spanish soldiers held sway in the area.

When the struggle for Mexican Independence began and was finally won, the Spanish soldiers were naturally withdrawn. Mines were abandoned and people fled to Tubac or Tucson to escape from Indian raids.

Until 1848, all of Arizona was a part of Mexico. Then in the treaty of Gudalupe Hidalgo, the United States gained all the land north of the Gila River. Later the Gadsden Purchase of 1853 acquired the rest of what is now Arizona. It must be remembered that for two hundred years the Spaniards held Arizona and the Southwest. Spanish courtesy and sense of leisure, fiestas, rodeos, etc., have all influenced Arizona's progress and culture.

During the Civil War, Arizona was in sympathy with the South. Many residents at the beginning of the Civil War were from the South. Shortly after hostilities began, the Federal government pulled all troops out of the area to fight in the East. Moreover, the United States Government issued a new mail contract to the Butterfield Overland Stage Company, permitting it to by-pass Arizona to the north. This event caused many Arizonans to feel as if the government in Washington had abandoned them. Without the protection of U. S. Troops, the mining and ranching activities of the area came to a standstill. Many were left to face the warring Indians tribes with really nothing but their own guns to protect them.

On August 1, 1861, Lieutenant-Colonel John R. Baylor and three hundred Texans seized Mesilla, New Mexico, in the name of the Confederacy. Mesilla was named the Confederate capital of the Southern Territory of New Mexico, which included all of Arizona and New Mexico, south of the 34th parallel from the Rio Grande to the Pacific Ocean. The only Civil War Battle to be fought in Arizona took place near the town of Red Rock at Picacho Pass. Actually it was more of a skirmish than a battle, with twelve Northern troops, led by Lieutenant Jame Barrett, fighting nine or ten Southern troops, led by Lieutenant Jack Swilling. The North suffered 6 casualties, 3 dead, including Lieutenant Barrett and three wounded. The Southern force had two wounded and 3 captured. The Northern victory marked the beginning of a strategic withdrawal of Confederate forces from Arizona.

Even though full records are not available in some instances, Arizona Indian groups at one time or another, to a greater or lesser degree, fought the Spanish, Mexicans, or Anglo-Americans, in an effort to maintain their cultural identities. Small, impoverished and isolated tribes, such as the Cocopah, Havasupai, Paiutes and Hopi were left alone and as a result had little or no conflict. But the fight and ferocity of the Apache is well known. For almost a quarter of a century and the expenditure of many millions of dollars, the American, the Apache and many other tribes fought each other and thousands of lives were lost.

In 1860 Arizona was a county of the New Mexico Territory with a total population of 6,482 according to the U. S. Census. This census lists only 2,442 of these as "Whites" and the rest, "Indians." Undoubtedly there were many more Indians in Arizona County than 4,040. These 4,040 must have been only those Indians who lived in or near communities and military establishments and who had peaceful commerce with the early settlers, traders, and soldiers.

The communities listed in the Census of 1860 were eight in number. This was the complete list, regardless of size, of all non-Indian settlements in Arizona. Tucson (pop. 915) is the only one of the eight that has maintained a prominent role. The others were: Gila City (pop. 150); San Xavier (pop. 200, of which 35 were "White"); Tubac (pop. 353, of which 310 were "White"); Patagonia (pop. 5); Ft. Mohave (pop. 130); Ft. Buchanan (pop. 142); and Maricopa Wells (pop. 53).

Arizona Territory was formed February 24, 1863, from the Western part of the New Mexico Territory. The newly formed territory had four counties: Mohave, Pima, Yavapai, and Yuma. Pah-Ute County was created from the Northern part of Mohave County in December 1865, but most of this county (12,225 square miles) was given to the State of Nevada in 1866. The remaining portion was returned to Mohave County.

A special Territorial Census was conducted in 1864. At that time the non-Indian population numbered 4,573. According to the U. S. Census of 1870, the Territory's population had grown to 9,658. The Arizona list of communities with population over 100 had grown to fourteen. Only four of these had been listed in the 1860 census: Tucson, Tubac, San Xavier, and Mohave City. Pima County of 1870 included part of present-day Pinal County so that the then new towns of Florence and Adamsville were listed in Pima County.

When Arizona became a Territory, Camp Whipple in Yavapai County was established as an Advance Army Post. Governor Goodwin said that the Territorial Capital should be near Ft. Whipple. Prescott came into existence in 1864 and soon was the Capital of Arizona Territory.

The decade from 1870 to 1880 was a period of great growth for Arizona Territory. Its 1880 population of 40,440 was over 300% greater than its 1870 population. Much of this population growth had occurred in the last few years of the decade concurrent with the advance of the two great railroads across the south and across the north of Arizona.

Arizona now was beginning to settle down into a modern culture. The last of the Apache troubles was settled in 1886. Permanent settlers and traders soon followed the miners to the rich silver discoveries, such as Globe and Tombstone, and established communities. The members of the Church of Jesus Christ of Latter Day Saints (Mormon) established colonies along the Little Colorado River and later penetrated deeper into Arizona creating permanent agricultural centers.

Shortly after the railroads were completed, a price war between the two railroads did even more to populate the West. In 1885 many people who wanted to move West but could not afford the regular fare, jumped at the chance to migrate at reduced rates. The two companies realized that neither could freeze out the other and stabilized fares at a price of $50. This was a great bargain and helped to bring about the greatest western migration since the Gold Rush Days. The majority of these immigrants went to California, but many stopped in Arizona or returned when they found California unsatisfactory.

By 1890 three more counties had been established, making a total of ten counties. The population of Arizona had grown to 88,243 — a ten-year increase of 118%. There were 35 cities and towns having a population over one-hundred in the 1890 Census of Arizona. It represented 15 newly reported towns and the dropping of 17 towns which had been listed in the 1880 census. The new towns appeared in mining areas where new discoveries had occurred, in cattle raising areas where the addition of railroads and the quelling of Apache Indian terror had benefited cattle raising, and along the northern route of the railroad. Of the 17 communities dropped, 12 were mining communities that died when the rich ore ran out, three were abandoned military posts, and two (Brigham City and Ehrenberg) were affected by the meandering of Arizona's rivers.

Many diverse factors affected economic growth during the 1890 decade. Early in the 1890's torrential rains flooded grazing lands and washed away topsoil. Resulting damage to range lands brought about heavy cattle losses. However, income derived from the industries of citrus production on a commercial basis, and the increased gold production resulting from the invention of the cyanide process for extracting gold from ore, tended to offset losses experienced in the cattle raising industry. The national financial panic in 1893 brought about devaluation of silver and the subsequent closing of many silver mines. The following year use of new processes for extracting copper revived the mining activity. Also during this decade, three major fires swept Jerome—the first in 1894, the second in 1898, and the third in 1899. It seems significant to note that the first long staple cotton was planted in 1899, a crop that has contributed greatly to the Arizona economy over the years.

The first decade of the Twentieth Century saw great growth in mining areas such as Globe, Jerome, and Bisbee, and considerable growth in cities along the railroads such as Winslow, Willcox, and Yuma. Copper production and development boomed throughout most of the first twenty-five years of the century, spurred on both by the demands of war industry and by improved technological processes. Some of the most notable occurrences from 1900 to 1910 include: the great Prescott fire in 1900, the railroad spur line to Grand Canyon in 1901, the incorporation of Salt River Valley Water Users Association in 1903 and its signing of the agreement to build Roosevelt Dam the following year, the forming of the Miami Copper Co. in 1906, the first large scale production from low-grade copper ores at Morenci in the same year, the prohibition of gambling in 1907, and the establishment of Grand Canyon as a national monument in 1908.

By 1910 Arizona's population had reached 204,354, an increase of 66% over 1900.

During the decade of 1910 to 1920 population continued to gain. The completion of Roosevelt Dam in 1911 and the subsequent availability of irrigation water greatly expanded agricultural development throughout the Salt River Valley. Later, dams and irrigation facilities on the Salt River and Verde River made it possible to open thousands of acres for cultivation. In 1910 the people of Arizona were pushing for statehood. The State Constitutional Convention was held in this year and the new State Constitution was ratified early the next year. Though Congress approved Arizona's constitution in 1911, President Taft vetoed admission until certain amendments were made. On February 14, 1912, Arizona was formally proclaimed the 48th State of the Union. Statehood did much to attract new pioneers and to develop all facets of the former Territory.

One of Arizona's pioneer luxury resorts, the San Marcos Hotel, built in 1910 at Chandler, was the forerunner of many luxury winter resorts to come to Central and Southern Arizona. The Camelback Inn, Mountain Shadows Resort, the Shangri-La Guest Ranch, all in Paradise Valley, are others.

Roosevelt Dam was dedicated on March 18, 1911. It was to supply the water for the future growth of metropolitan Phoenix.

The first large scale copper flotation process plant in the United States was built in Inspiration.

In 1919, the State's first commercial aviation company was formed in Tucson.

By 1920 the population had grown to 334,162 — a 63% increase during the preceding ten years. The impetus gained during the war carried into the first year of the new decade, but the postwar depression had a dampening effect on Arizona's fabulous growth in population, industry, commerce, and agriculture. Phoenix College was established in 1920 and the State Legislature passed the State's first Workmen's Compensation Act in that year. In 1924 the Southwestern National Monuments Office was created to protect and administer some of the scenic and historical monuments.

Toward the middle of the decade economic progress resumed a rapid pace. Transportation got a boost with the completion of a modern highway from Yuma to El Centro in 1925 and with the opening of the first scheduled commercial air service in 1926. The Mormon Temple, an imposing structure in Mesa, was completed in 1927; and Coolidge Dam, additional insurance against drought, was finished the next year. The stock market crash of 1929 was not felt immediately in Arizona, but the effects were not long in coming and there was little optimism as the decade drew to a close.

The Great Depression of the 1930's brought acute suffering to Arizona. Though the State was slow to feel the severest effects when compared with Eastern states, it was also slow to recover. Arizona's population continued to grow throughout the depression, although its rate of increase became less than at any other time in history. Even as early in the depression as 1930, Arizona's population of 435,573 represented an increase of only 30% over the 1920 figure.

The following ten years showed a rate of growth of less than half that percentage. Most mines closed and the few that operated worked on greatly reduced payrolls. Farm prices fell to almost nothing. Construction ceased and what little manufacturing there had been in the State disappeared. Very few people in the United States had enough money to go touring or vacationing to Arizona; therefore, many resorts and places of recreation closed or operated with a skeleton staff. Many of the immigrants to Arizona were refugees from other parts of the country, grateful for a warm winter climate if for nothing else. Thousands of unemployed boys were brought in to the twenty-seven CCC Camps established in Arizona. The conservation projects performed by these boys were of great benefit to Arizona, as many projects were accomplished that the State could not have afforded for many years. Mining and agriculture slowly began to crawl upward in 1936, but only mining made any real progress until World War II.

The population in 1940 was 499,261, an increase of only 15% over the 435,573 of 1930. The new spurt of growth in Arizona's business and population due to the war did not begin until 1942 when the prices of meat, copper, cotton, and other commodities shot upward. Many military air bases and other training centers were established throughout the State, bringing thousands of servicemen and their families to Arizona. The relatively protected situation of Arizona, its year-round mild climate, and the opportunity it afforded for industrial dispersement, brought industrial plants with government contracts into the State, establishing Arizona's potential for manufacturing. Many of the workers and owners of these plants were anxious to stay in Arizona after the war was over, and many servicemen who had been stationed here returned after release from the service. Though population losses occurred from 1943 to 1945, by 1946 more than 100,000 G.I.'s and their families had made Arizona their home. Many other postwar arrivals were people who had planned to retire in Arizona when the war was over. They invested in land or industries, adding to Arizona's capital growth.

During World War II many major employers of the United States established operations in Arizona. Early during the wartime period the Navajo Ordnance Depot was established at Bellemont. Consolidated Vultee brought its operation to the Tucson area in 1943 and operated until cessation of hostilities in 1945. The aluminum plant in Maricopa County, just outside Phoenix at that time, was operated by Aluminum Company of America (Alcoa) from 1943 through 1946. AiResearch, a division of Garrett Corporation, operated a facility in Phoenix from 1942 through 1946. Also during the period, Goodyear Aircraft was very active in the Phoenix area. While many of these firms ceased operation at the end of hostilities, it is interesting to note that the same facilities were rapidly activated either during the period between World War II and the Korean Conflict or early during the rearmament period of the Korean outbreak.

During the postwar period the initial installation of Motorola was established in the Phoenix area. Also prior to 1950, Reynolds Aluminum Company reactivated the War Assets Administration plant near Phoenix that had been operated by Alcoa. This plant became one of the world's largest aluminum extrusion plants under one roof.

During the decade of the 1950's Arizona's population and economic growth, though war-inspired, had been proven to be not war-dependent. The population of the State reached 749,587 in 1950, an increase of more than 50% over that of 1940. This great increase of population was effective in causing tremendous growth in construction and trade, as well as increases in other branches of the economy. Manufacturing, although it had grown from practically nothing to an employment of almost 10% of the total, was only crawling compared to its future tremendous expansion during the 1950's. Changes in the tax laws and planned programs to bring manufacturing into the State were so successful early in the 1950's, that it became Arizona's major source of income by 1956. Cattle, cotton, and vegetable prices remained good and income from tourism was excellent in this period.

The 1950's was the period of the greatest industrial expansion that Arizona had experienced since statehood. Perhaps in terms of percentage growth rates, the early Territorial days outstripped the 1950's, but numerical growth incidental to the Korean outbreak and persistent growth since the end of the conflict, have caused the 1950's to be called by many, "Arizona's period of economic emergence."

Although World War II had seen many successful manufacturing establishments operated in this State, their existence was due primarily to military expediency. The advantages of excellent flying weather, location away from congested areas, and available labor supply had far outweighed economic reasons that would have prevented location of manufacturing and processing industries in this State. During the 1950's, however, Arizona was "discovered" by many major manufacturing establishments. AiResearch, which had had a very successful history in Phoenix during World War II, reestablished a plant in the Phoenix area in 1951. Since that date AiResearch has continued to expand until it can be said that AiResearch of Phoenix is the Nation's largest job-shop-machine-shop and the nation's largest manufacturer of small gas turbine equipment. Early in 1951 Hughes

Aircraft chose Tucson as the site for its guided missile manufacturing establishments. Hughes also expanded rapidly and in recent years has maintained stable employment in the Pima County area. Infilco Corporation, a world-renowned manufacturer of water treatment and sewage treatment equipment, established their plant in Tucson in 1950.

Firms that were established and operated as a result of the Korean Conflict included the Grand Central Aircraft Company in Tucson, which operated from 1950 through 1954 modifying propeller and later jet powered aircraft. The same physical plant was selected late in 1954 as the site of an aircraft modification and test flight center by Douglas Aircraft. This firm operated in the Tucson area until the revised Military Expenditure Program forced closure early in 1960. The Phoenix Parachute Company was established in 1951 and operated, with minor ups and downs in employment, through 1954. Other small operations, many of which represented nationally known firms, found sites for successful wartime production in the State of Arizona.

In 1951 the Yuma Test Station was established as a proving ground for Army equipment. Many of the modern weapons that found their way to the battlefields of Korea and Vietnam, or that are now in our arsenal of defense, were first developed and tested at this modern facility.

Fort Huachuca, as a frontier cavalry outpost, as a permanent infantry and cavalry station during World War I, as a division training post during World War II, and as a training base for ground troop aviation engineers for Korea, has had a profound influence on the history of the Southwest since its establishment in 1877. In January of 1954, Army Headquarters announced that Fort Huachuca would be converted into the Army's major electronic proving ground. With Fort Huachuca established as the major proving ground of Army electronic equipment, Arizona became, in the eyes of many of the Nation's major electronics equipment producers, an area well worthy of consideration for plant location. The growth of the electronics components industry in Arizona has been virtually unparalleled in any other part of our nation. In 1955 Motorola Corporation announced the establishment of a second plant, followed by the announcement in 1956 of the establishment of a third plant. Also in 1956 the General Electric Corporation announced that Phoenix had been selected as the site for its computer division. In 1955 Sperry Rand Corporation announced that manufacturing establishments would be located in the Phoenix area. Other smaller local plants also have grown tremendously in the electronic components manufacturing field during the period 1950 to 1960.

Aircraft and electronic equipment were not the only types of manufacturing employment growing in the State of Arizona during the decade of the '50's. Garment manufacturing plants found a healthy labor market and a welcome reception, with particular emphasis on the period subsequent to 1952. Prior to 1952 only a few hundred persons found employment in the garment trades in this State. Near the end of 1960 almost 2,000 persons were so employed.

Naturally, with considerable population growth and gains in manufacturing, construction scored major levels of progress during the period. Construction of highways, residences, commercial buildings, factories, and warehouses was at an all-time high during the period of the '50's. In 1956, however, perhaps one of the largest construction projects ever to be announced in the United States was awarded for an Arizona site. At that time announcement was made of the Glen Canyon Dam Project. This project, located in upper Coconino County, involved the building of one of the nation's largest hydroelectric and water storage dams in a location very remote from population, labor force, or construction materials. As a result, an entire new town — Page, Arizona — was established.

By 1960 in the State of Arizona, population was spurred onward by economic growth and had attained a level of 1,302,161. This represented an increase of 74% over the preceding ten years. The 1950's showed the most rapid percentage increase of any decade since the fabulous 1880's. It must be remembered that in the 1880's the railroads were completed to and through Arizona, allowing the ultimate development of the area. In 100 years Arizona has grown from a population of 6,482 to 1,302,161.

The Democratic Party dominated the politics of the new State until after the Second World War. The newcomers saw in the Republican Party an alternative to the entrenched Democrats. In 1950, Howard Pyle became the third Republican governor since statehood. Barry Goldwater led the maturing Republicans to a 1952 Senatorial victory, defeating Senate Majority Leader Ernest McFarland. Goldwater became a national figure for the conservative cause and eventually the Presidential nominee for the Republican Party in 1964.

In elections Arizona has a closed primary, with crossover voting prohibited. Democrats vote for Democrats and Republicans vote for Republicans. In 1986, figures released by Secretary of State Rose Mofford show that there were 702,274 Republicans, 669,741 Democrats, and 176,741 independents and others, for a total of 1,548,259. Tucson has a history of voting Democratic while Phoenix favors the Republican party.

Arizona has six congressional districts.

* 1st District, which includes parts of east Phoenix and the east Valley.

* 2nd District, which includes parts of south and west Phoenix, extends to Yuma, south to Nogales, and takes in the western half of Tucson.

* 3rd District, which takes in parts of west and northwest Phoenix and extends to the northwestern corner of the state.

* 4th District, which includes parts of north and northeast Phoenix and extends to the northeastern corner of the state.

* 5th District, which takes in the eastern side of Tucson and extends to the southeastern corner of the state.

* Because of growth Arizona will have a sixth district in 1992. A new congressperson will be elected.

It is to be noted that Arizona has many military installations and retired military. These blocks of votes usually lean toward the Republican party in Arizona. Sun City, the world's famous retirement center, usually favors Republican candidates in most elections.

In 1991 voter registration in Arizona bodes well for the GOP in the future. A Republican governor was elected and Maricopa County, the largest population county in the state, boosted its republican registration almost two to one over the Democrats.

CHAPTER 6.

Steamboats on the Colorado

"No one liked the camels in Arizona. Assuredly they could carry much water and much heavier loads than a mule. They were much speedier, and were infinitely more two footed. Unfortunately they had one social problem that far outweighed all of their assets. Quite literally they stunk."

David Rees

Steamboats are seldom mentioned in stories of the early West. Yet for more than a half-century the Colorado River furnished the avenue of Commerce for river towns, mines, and at times, for the railroads themselves.

The 1870's were the heyday of the river traffic with over 100 men employed. Before 1890 the number had dwindled to less than 40 and the last boats stopped running around 1917. Their last stand seems to have been the short haul from Yuma to the mining town of Picacho.

In their day, however, the Colorado River steamers not only answered a distinct, economic need but wrote another colorful chapter in the West's history. Boilers and stamps for the mills at Prescott, La Paz and El Dorado were brought up river on fleet, vessels so built, that they "could float in a heavy dew" and frequently had to, for the errant Colorado would leave a mud bank today right in the spot of yesterday's channel.

The first river steamers came in the holds of sailing ships from San Francisco, but soon Yankee ingenuity went to work and the bulk of the river fleet was built on the spot with only the boilers and engines imported. One of the world's most unique shipyards served the river. It was at Port Isabel, Mexico. It isn't on any map today but Port Isabel itself was a phenomenon. It was an American town built on the east bank of the river at the mouth — far down in Sonora, Mexico. Steamers were built, repaired and rebuilt at this unique town. Also unusual was the drydock at the shipyard. It was made by scooping out a trough in the silt. A steamer would be run in at high tide. There is a rise and fall of 22 feet, so at low tide the ship was high and dry. A mule team would take a scarper and build a dike back of the ship and there you had a dry dock.

When the steamer was ready for service again, the process was reversed. Other things at Port Isabel were different, too. The company warehouse was the hull of the old Cocopah, hauled up and its decks enclosed with shiplap.

In the 1860's the river boats were often run by rivals but in May, 1877, the Southern Pacific reached the California side of the river and soon thereafter, bought out the private steamer concerns. "The Pacific Tourist Guide," of 1879 announced:

"The steamers of the Colorado Steam Navigation Company leave Yuma weekly from January 1 to November 1, and during November and December, every alternate Saturday.
Steamers leave for Camp Mojave every fifth week and continue to El Dorado Canyon from May 1 to November 1 if the weather permits.
Yuma to Castle Dome, 35 miles with $5 fare; Ehrenburg, 125 miles, $15; Aubrys, 220 miles, $28; Camp Mojave, 300 miles, $35; Hardyville, 312 miles, $35; Dorado Canyon, 365 miles, $45."

It is reported that when the Yuma Indians saw the steamboat, they were terrified and ran crying that the devil was coming up the river blowing fire out his nose.

The early day pilots would have a hard time recognizing their river today. Civilization has harnessed the river of the West and, in so doing, has thrown six dams across it between Lake Mead and the international line. There are Laguna and the Imperial Dams, north of Yuma, where irrigation water is diverted for the Imperial Valley; Head Gate Rock Dam near Parker and Parker Dam, a few miles upstream; Davis Dam above Needles; and finally Hoover Dam.

The man-made lakes behind these barriers have buried landmarks, old towns and the sites of the early day wharves. In other places the shifting channel has left old ports high and dry two or three miles from the present river.

Much of the colorful early history of Arizona is concerned with river navigation, which was a matter of skill and experience since there are constant difficulties and dangers to overcome. Sometimes at the mouth of the great stream tidal waves raged through the delta. Other problems in the lower river were shallows, concealed mud, and sandbars; farther up the river were hidden pebble bars and submerged boulders. At times boats were grounded for days.

Upstream traffic carried general merchandise, mining and milling machinery, foods, and miscellaneous items, passengers, troops and military troop supplies. The down river loads consisted of bullion, ores, hides, pelts, wood, passengers, and troops. Each river town was a terminus of freight route; the principal points above Yuma were Ehrenberg for shipments to and from Wickenburg, and Hardyville for Prescott. Callville, the Mormon settlement on the Colorado a few miles below the Virgin River, was first reached by barge in 1866. It soon became an important shipping center for wagon transportation as far as Salt Lake City.

By 1850 activity around the junction of the Gila and Colorado Rivers had increased to such an extent that General Persifer Smith sent Lt. George H. Derby to make reconnaissance of the Colorado, from its mouth to Fort Yuma, with an idea of establishing a river route from the Gulf of California to the military reservation. If this could be accomplished, it would be possible to bring supplies from San Diego and San Francisco, much more cheaply than they could be brought by land over the desert route from the coast.

Derby and his party in the schooner, Invincible, under the command of Capt. Wilcox, arrived at the mouth of the Colorado in 1851. Because of the shallowness of the water, they could ascend the stream only about 24 miles. At this point the flatboats were used for another 60 miles. By then the expedition clearly showed the feasibility of the river route, and it was adopted immediately.

In the spring of 1851 another schooner, the Sierra Madre, under the command of George A. Johnson, arrived at the river's mouth with supplies for the troops at the fort. Shortly thereafter Ben Hartshorn, Capt. Wilcox, and George Johnson made a contract with the federal government to bring stores from the schooners to Fort Yuma. The waters were so shallow about the mouth of the river that it was necessary to transfer all goods to barges and then tow the barges. This was the beginning of a profitable river trade on the Colorado.

Soon the Hartshorn, Wilcox, and Johnson Company became the Colorado Steam Navigation Company. Although this new concern did not own a single boat when formed, it immediately purchased one that Capt. Turnbull had brought from San Francisco to the head of the Gulf. There the steamer was torn down, shipped to Robinson's Landing at Yuma, re-assembled, and named the Uncle Sam. She was sixty-five feet long, sixteen feet wide, and 3½ feet deep. Like most river craft of those days, she was a side wheeler, powered by a locomotive boiler of twenty horsepower. After 3½ years of service between the mouth of the river, and Yuma, the Uncle Sam sank at her mooring at Pilot Knob, nine miles west of Yuma.

In 1854 Capt. Johnson, one of the navigation firm members, brought the steamer General Jessup to Yuma. This being her maiden voyage, she carried thirty-five tons of freight although her capacity was sixty tons in two feet of water. She was one hundred and four feet long, seventeen feet wide, and was powered by two fifty horse power engines. The General Jessup was the first steampowered craft to ascend above Yuma when she carried mining supplies some twenty miles above Hardyville in 1858.

In 1854 the U.S. Government paid 75 dollars a ton for transporting supplies from the mouth of the Colorado to Fort Yuma. The freight bill for 14 months amounted to $94,000.

Johnson later headed the exploration party of 1857, in the General Jessup. Of the latter trip he wrote:

> "In December, 1857, I left Fort Yuma with the steamer General Jessup for the purpose of determining the navigability of the Colorado above Yuma. Captain William A. Winder was in charge. My crew consisted of an assistant pilot, fourteen or fifteen deck hands, and six mountain men and trappers. Our trip was attended by no particular difficulties.
>
> Late in December I arrived at a canyon in the Colorado which was not navigable. This was about seventy-five miles above Fort Mojave. At this point is the mouth of a canyon which comes in from the west known as El Dorado. Knowing I had reached the height of practical navigation, I turned back.
>
> The next day I landed on the east bank for wood. While lying there an expedition came in sight which proved to be that of Gen. E. F. Beale."

While making a trip to the mining camp of Pichacho, the General Jessup, struck a submerged boulder and sank. Fortunately, the Colorado Navigation Company had another seaworthy ship called the Colorado Number One. This vessel was dispatched to the assistance of the ill-fated General Jessup. Eventually, the sunken craft was raised and towed to Yuma for repairs. Some months later she returned to service. The unlucky schooner finally came to an end when one of her boilers exploded while she was running the rapids near Ogden's Landing, about 25 miles above Lerdo Colony, which is a few miles above the mouth of the river. Two men were killed in the explosion and the boat was condemned. Her machinery was removed and shipped to San Francisco; her hull was towed to Menturn Slough and sunk.

The Colorado Number Two was constructed at the Yuma ship yards during the Civil War. She was the fifth vessel to be put in service by The Colorado Steam Navigation Co. The shipyard at Port Isabel was the more popular place for repairing and building vessels, but great caution was taken in erecting the Colorado Number Two, because of the fear that a Confederate Cruiser might invade the waters around Port Isabel and destroy the ship before it was completed.

The Colorado Number Two, like her predecessor the Colorado Number One, was put into service on the river and navigated between the river's mouth and points as far north as Fort Mojave, which was over two hundred miles north of Yuma. In March, 1878, she was taken into the shipyards and given a complete overhaul. This was done by taking out every defective plank from her bottom and replacing them with new ones. Her seams were re-caulked and pitched, and her bottom painted with coal tar. Also due to the presence of a great deal of driftwood on the water's surface, the ship's bottom was fitted out with large knobs under her counters for future protection against the menace.

After faithfully serving her owner for over 15 years, the Colorado Number Two went to the bottom of the muddy stream. Her haul was moved out at Port Isabel and used as a foundation for a large warehouse, which later burned and nearly destroyed the entire port. Her machinery, being still in good condition, was dismantled and shipped to San Francisco, where it was later used on the Hattie Picket, a steamer plying the Sacramento River.

A competitive boat line came into existence on the Colorado River when the surrounding regions experienced a mining boom about 1858. This new company was founded by Captain T. E. Trueworthy, owner of the steamer, *Esmeraldo*, which had been navigated from San Francisco to Port Isabel under the command of Captain C. C. Overman. Captain Trueworthy had been operating a steamship business on the Sacramento River before coming to the Colorado region in 1861. In this year he purchased the steamer, Nina Tilden, in San Francisco and organized the Pacific Colorado Navigation Company.

The new competing steamboat line lasted only about 6 years. The end came in 1867 when the Colorado Steam Navigation Company purchased the steamers Esmeraldo and Nina Tilden, and the barges Black Crook and White Fawn.

After selling out to the Colorado Steam Navigation Company, Capt. Trueworthy invested a small fortune in another sailing venture. He converted a large 182 foot Sacramento River barge into a four masted schooner, and christened the craft the Victoria. The intention of the owner was to load her with lumber, sail to China and construct barges for use on the Yang Tse River. But instead of going to the Orient, the Victoria, under the command of C. E. Qualin, left San Francisco for the mouth of the Colorado River with 4,000,000 feet of lumber, 50 tons of groceries and 800 barrels of whiskey. Her voyage from the seacoast port was uneventful and she anchored 25 miles up the river. While riding at anchor there a strong, incoming tide caused her to drift over her own anchor, and a protruding fluke tore a hole in her bottom. The ship stayed afloat, probably because she carried 4,000,000 feet of lumber; later she was towed to Starvation Point, about 125 miles south of Yuma, and tied near the bank. There the Indians for some unknown reason, set fire to the weeds and underbrush. The flames rapidly spreading, finally reached the Victoria. The groceries were saved, the lumber was set free and floated out to sea, but the whiskey is reported to be resting on the bottom of the river. This catastrophe nearly ruined Captain Trueworthy financially.

The Colorado Steam Navigation Company was very prosperous from the day it started business. At one time there were 12 steamers and as many barges operating on the river between its mouth and Yuma and points north of Yuma. Except the mining supplies and a few necessities for the Fort at Mojave, most of the freight was taken off the steamers at Yuma and reshipped by mule teams to all parts of Arizona and cities in Sonora, Mexico.

The barges used in the river trade played almost as prominent a part as the steamers which towed them. The barge, Black Crook, was the first to bring freight to Yuma. She was 128 feet long and 28 feet wide, and was constructed at the river's mouth in 28 days by Charley Overman, Charley Tyson, and Jack Mellon. The White Fawn was built in 1864, and lengthened in 1867. She was constructed in San Francisco, sent in pieces and assembed at Port Isabel.

In 1867 the barge, Pumpkin Seed, loaded with iron, was moored to Jaeger's Landing in Yuma, when a heavy rain came and filled her, causing her to sink.

During all these early years when the steamboat company was operating, the offices occupied four rooms in an old adobe building along the river's edge in Yuma. It was in this building that the various boat captains and construction experts were called together to plan new river crafts as fast as the trade demanded them.

The people of the Yuma area had sent numerous petitions to Congress asking aid in making the river safer for navigation; and in 1870 a sum of money was appropriated to purchase a steam barge for dredging. This craft was brought to Yuma, where it caused much commotion because of a rumor that it was a Mexican gunboat, flying the American flag. The barge was used for several years in dredging above Needles, California, and greatly helped navigation on the river. It was later sold to an individual by the name of Whitcombe, who used it for a pleasure barge.

Navigation on the Colorado River was not all pleasure, but it was not all grief.

When the weather was cool many of the trips were very enjoyable and scenic. It is recorded that the steamer, Cocopa, made a roundtrip from Hardyville to Camp El Dorado, a distance of about one hundred and twenty miles, in a little less than 24 hours.

In 1874 a distance of two hundred miles consumed 11 days by stage coach. The pleasure trip experienced by Hardy was far different from what Mrs. Martha Summerhayes endured while going from Fort Yuma to Mojave.

Mrs. Summerhayes and her husband, a lieutenant in the army, sailed up the river on the Gila which was loaded with supplies and towed a barge full of soldiers. The thermometer varied from one hundred seven to one hundred twenty-two in the shade. Even at night it was impossible to sleep in the staterooms. Mrs. Summerhayes described the situation as follows:

"And thus began another day of intolerable glare and heat ... There was nothing to relieve the monotony of the scenery. On each side of us, low river banks, and nothing between those and the horizon line ... at last on the 8th of September, we arrived at Fort Mohave, 11 days from Fort

Yuma. 'A quick trip,' said the Captain. I listened and wondered if I had heard right, for those 11 days in mid-summer on the Great Colorado had burned themselves into my memory."

In 1858 Lt. Joseph C. Ives was steaming up the Colorado River in an iron boat, called the Explorer, for the purpose of determining whether or not the stream was navigable. With much pushing and towing, the clumsy craft finally reached Black Canyon and then almost met with disaster near the spot where Hoover Dam is located. Following the exploratory trip, the boat was sold and then disappeared from the pages of history. Within recent years the craft had been rediscovered, almost buried in the silt of the Colorado River delta — and its skeleton is still to be seen there. Here is one part of the story about one of the most thrilling episodes in the history of the Southwest:

"We were shooting past the entrance to Black Canyon," wrote Lieutenant Joseph C. Ives in his mariner's log book on March 8, 1858, "when the Explorer with a stunning crash, brought up abruptly and instantaneously against a sunken rock. For a second the impression was that the canyon had fallen in. The concussion was so violent that the men near the bow were thrown overboard; the doctor, Mr. Mollhausen and myself, having been seated in front of the upper deck, were precipitated head foremost into the bottom of the boat; the fireman who was pitching a log into the fire, went halfways in with it; the boiler was thrown out of place; the steam pipe doubled up; the wheelhouse was torn away, and it was expected the boat would fill in and sink instantly by all . . ."

Thus ended, after three and one-half months of arduous labor, the initial cruise of the Explorer, the iron steamboat commissioned by the U. S. War Dept. in 1857, to determine whether or not the Colorado River was a navigable stream.

The Explorer was built in Philadelphia. It was a 56 foot stern-wheel steamer. After a brief trial run on the Delaware River, it was knocked down in eight sections, shipped by boat overland to the Pacific, again by boat to San Francisco, and finally to the mud flats at the head of the Gulf of California, to be assembled for the trip up the river as far as it would go.

It was built of iron, with a huge boiler mounted in the center of the deck. The boiler was too heavy. To correct this weakness and give the craft longitudinal stability, four long wooden beams were bolted to the bottom. Needless to say, this clumsy make-shift creature caused no end of trouble in navigating the countless bars in the channel of the lower Colorado.

Accompanying Lt. Ives on the expedition were A. J. Carrol of Philadelphia as engineer; Dr. J. S. Newberry, physician and geologist; F. W. Egolffstein, who had been a member of the Fremont expedition in 1853, topographer; P. H. Taylor and meteorological assistants; H. B. Mollhausen, artist and collector in natural history. Lt. Tipton, 3rd artillery, and 25 soldiers from the garrison at Yuma served as military escort. Due to the limited capacity of the boat, the soldiers traveled overland with pack-train. It was an escort in name only, since the troops left Yuma several days after the Explorer steamed away, and did not catch up with the river expedition until Ives reached Mojave Valley on his return trip.

Lt. Ives completed the reconnaissance without serious mishap, and on the basis of his report to Secretary of War, John F. Floyd in 1869, the Colorado was declared to be a navigable stream.

A few months after the return of the expedition the Explorer was sold by the government to Yuma rivermen who planned to use it for freighting on the Colorado. According to old Arizona records quoted by Godfrey Sykes in his book, "The Colorado Delta," after a few trips hauling wood, the steamer broke away from its moorings near Pilot Knob, floated downstream and disappeared from sight. Thus ended the first chapter in the saga of the good ship Explorer. Seventy years passed. The men who had piloted the Explorer and stoked mesquite wood in its huge boiler, remained as living names only to those students of history who had read the fine record left by Lt. Ives.

Then in 1929 word came out of the mesquite and willow jungle that covers the delta of the Colorado, that an aged Indian named Calabasa, had seen the rusted hulk of an old barge partly buried in the silt of a channel long abandoned by the fickle waters of the Colorado.

The story of the white man's rediscovery of this boat was told by Gus Seligman, member of an engineering party engaged in surveying the Colorado Delta. Seligman, covered nearly every foot of the vast silt plain by car, horseback or on foot. He said:

"Tony, my brother, Dirk, and I later found the remains of the boat, early in 1929. We took pictures of it and began to look up its history. About six months later, C. N. Perry joined us in our work, identified the craft as Ives' Explorer, and wrote an article about it for the American Society of Civil Engineers.

At the time we found the boat there wasn't much left. It reminded me of a carcass after the coyotes and buzzards were through with it. Only the bones remained."

By 1878 when the railroad bridged the Colorado at Yuma, the steamers Mohave and Gila were the oldest boats in operation. These had been in service for 20 years. In order to prevent any competition, the Southern Pacific Railroad bought out the Colorado Steam Navigation Company in the same year it bridged the river.

The river trade decreased considerably after the coming of the railroad, but several steamers were built either at the Yuma shipyards or at Port Isabel, Mexico, during the eighties. These were known as the Searchlight, Cochan, and St. Valier. The Searchlight happened to be above Laguna Dam when it was completed in 1900, and had to be lifted over the structure by the government.

The other great river in Arizona is the Gila. Many years before Columbus came to the Americas, thousands of people lived along the Gila. In particular, three cultures dominated the Gila area. They are The Anasazi, the Hohokam and the Mogollon. Their greatest achievement was the invention of the atlatl, or spear thrower.

The Gila has its beginnings in the Mogollon Mountains and runs the width of the state. It flows into the Colorado River at the famed Yuma Crossing. It is about 600 miles long and it certainly was the center of much of the history in this state. Many people followed its path on the way to California. It had many names such as: Totonteac, River of the name of Jesus, Blue, Blaufuss, Poison, Helay, River of the Sun and River of the Apostles. As an institution, it was the bread and butter of Arizona.

It is to be noted that people have been living along the Gila for about 25 thousand years. Hence, people were living there before they were living in any of the other 49 states. Numerous ball courts were excavated along the Gila showing that the early settlers played some kind of a game like soccer. A rubber ball was found by archaeologists and it is now in the Southwest Museum in Los Angeles. Research has found about 50 ball courts along the Gila and it seems to tell us that the people had a high degree of civilization. Games seem to indicate a higher degree of culture and leisure than the nomad cultures of other peoples.

CHAPTER 7.

Mining

"There are two poisonous spiders in Arizona. They are the black widow and the brown recluse. They both enjoy locating in such fly-infested places as outdoor privies. People using these toilets, unaware that they are invading the sanctuary of these normally shy spiders, have been bitten in the most sensitive and unmentionable places."

Marshall Trimble
in his book, ARIZONA

The history of Arizona is inextricably tied to mining. From the earliest days, silver mines had been worked by the Spanish whenever there were sufficient troops to provide protection against the Apaches. The Mowry and Heintzelman Silver Mines near Patagonia and Tubac in Santa Cruz County were being worked in the late 1850's. The rich gold placer deposits along the Gila and Colorado Rivers were discovered in 1858, and the gold placers on the Hassayampa and Lynx Creeks were located in 1863. Henry Wickenburg discovered the Vulture Mine in 1863. This mine was the most productive of Arizona's early gold mines. The Peoples Party made a rich find at Antelope Hill near present-day Yarnell; and a little later all of these rich strikes not only brought in a tremendous influx of miners, but also helped to build a solid foundation for Arizona commerce and demonstrated the Territory's value to the Union. To keep these riches for the U. S. Treasury, Congress was impelled to grant Arizona separate territorial status in 1863 and detail sufficient troops to hold it against the Confederacy.

The prospectors who joined the great rush to Arizona after the Civil War, did such a thorough job that most of Arizona's primary mineral discoveries were made from 1865 to 1880. These included not only the Silver King and Silver Queen Mines, but also all the richest copper deposits including those at Clifton-Morenci, Globe, Ray, Bisbee, and Jerome. Prior to 1870, however, copper was not important as the demand was not sufficient to pay for complicated processing and high transportation costs.

41

Silver on top and copper below is a common occurrence in Arizona so that many present-day copper mines originally were worked only for silver.

The passage of the Sherman Silver Purchase Act in 1890 demonetizing silver, along with the fact that the richest and most easily obtainable ore in the mines was nearly exhausted. It brought an end to silver mining by 1900, except as a by-product. Gold mining, however, continued to be a significant factor in Arizona's economy until after World War I. The postwar depression in 1921 drastically reduced gold mining activities until 1932, when there was a small upswing which lasted until the gold mine closing order in 1942. Since then Arizona's gold production has consisted only of that produced as a by-product of the mining of other metals.

The earliest copper mine to produce in Arizona was at Ajo. It had such extremely rich ore that a small profit could be made in spite of the tremendous costs of shipping the ore by mule train to the Gulf, where it was loaded on ships and sent to the nearest smelter in Swansea, Wales. The Ajo Mine was worked on this basis from 1855 to 1861, after which the ore was no longer rich enough to make this method of mining profitable.

By the 1870's, industrialists, capitalists, and miners were beginning to sense the potential importance of copper. All the fairly rich deposits were developed in this period and smelters were built to handle the bonanza copper ores of the time. In 1886 the first concentrator which made lower grade, porphyry ores profitable was built at Morenci. From that time on, as richness of the ore declined, the copper industry compensated by inventing new methods for profitable mining.

In 1908 Arizona became the Nation's top producer of copper. It lost first place in 1909 to Montana but regained it in 1910 and has held it ever since.

The postwar depression closed most of Arizona's mines in 1921; but they recovered rapidly, reopened in 1922, and did well until the depression following the stock market crash of 1929. By 1932 all of them had either reduced operations to a bare minimum essential for maintenance or had closed entirely. Not one of the State's major mining corporations failed during this period, and beginning in 1935 most of the mines reopened and production was gradually increased by the mining of low-grade ores through open-pit operation. In 1939 signs of impending conflict in Europe became unmistakable and Arizona's Legislature, recognizing the great demands that war would make on Arizona's mining industry, created the Arizona Department of Mineral Resources to aid the industry in every way possible. After December 7, 1941, the United States acted to spur copper production by offering loans and premium prices to developers of marginal ore deposits and over-quota premiums to owners of established mines which increased their production. These incentives, together with the reduction of available manpower and man-hour production, accelerated efforts to devise ways and means by which machine power could be utilized to produce copper.

New drilling and blasting techniques, full-revolving electric shovels, and diesel locomotives are a few examples of the numerous innovations which were introduced to improve production and efficiency of mining operations. Federal Government assistance made possible the exploration of low-grade deposits and the very expensive preparation of properties for the use of block-caving mining methods. The development of simplified mill machinery enabled mill operators to use women workers partially to relieve the manpower shortage.

Contrary to pessimistic predictions, the end of World War II in 1945, did not bring a reduction in the need for copper and other Arizona metals. The pent-up domestic demand for products unavailable during the war, coupled with the "Cold War" arms race and the Korean Conflict in 1950, actually called for an increase in metal production.

The mining industry continues to play a vital part in Arizona's economy.

Copper annually accounts for approximately 85% of all minerals produced in Arizona. Moreover, the output of most other metals largely is a by product of copper mining. Sand and gravel are the largest non-metallic minerals produced locally.

Arizona is rich in coal. Geologists claim the state has enough coal deposits for its energy needs to last for 100 years.

Arizona is also blessed with tremendous salt deposits around Glendale, Phoenix, Kingman, Eloy and Tucson. Of all the deposits, only the West Glendale area is currently being mined. Nearly 1 million tons of salt have been excavated there in the past 12 years.

MINERALS BY COUNTY

County	Principal Minerals Produced in Each County
Apache	Petroleum, helium, clays, pumice, sand and gravel, natural gas, stone.
Cochise	Copper, stone, lime, sand and gravel, gold, silver.
Coconino	Pumice, sand and gravel, stone.
Gila	Copper, lime, stone, asbestos, sand and gravel, silver, gold, molybdenum, clays.
Graham	Sand and gravel, copper, pumice.
Greenlee	Copper, lime, silver, gold, stone, sand and gravel.
Maricopa	Sand and gravel, lime, stone, clays, mica, salt.
Mohave	Copper, molybdenum, sand and gravel, silver, feldspar, gold, stone.
Navajo	Coal, sand and gravel, iron ore, pumice, stone.
Pima	Copper, molybdenum, cement, silver, sand and gravel, stone, gold, lime, lead, clays, zinc, mica.
Pinal	Copper, molybdenum, gold, silver, sand and gravel, lime, gypsum, stone, perlite, pyrites, clays.
Santa Cruz	Zinc, sand and gravel, lead, stone.
Yavapai	Copper, cement, zinc, sand and gravel, molybdenum, stone, lime, silver, gypsum, lead, clays, gold, pumice.
Yuma	Sand and gravel, stone, lead, silver, gold, zinc, tungsten.

CHAPTER 8.

The Executive and Legislative Branches

No one should criticize his state or country unless he is willing to dedicate himself to public service to make it better. It is easy to criticize; it is most difficult to give of oneself for others.

Robert Rink

The Constitution of the State of Arizona disperses executive power and responsibility by creating a plural executive consisting of governor, secretary of state, state auditor, treasurer, attorney general, and superintendent of public instruction. These six officials, according to the constitution, make up the executive department; but in reality they head an executive branch consisting of numerous other administrative officers, boards, commissions, and agencies established by statute. The constitution also provides specifically for an elective corporation commission of three members, an elective mine inspector, a state examiner appointed by the governor, and a state board of education and a board of regents which are partly ex-officio and partly appointive.

In harmony with the theory that divides executive power, the constitution fixes four-year terms for the six officers who head the executive branch. All are eligible for re-election for an indefinite number of terms, with the exception of the treasurer, who cannot "succeed himself . . . for the succeeding two years after the expiration of the term for which he shall have been elected." In view of the scanty discretionary power lodged in the treasurer, this ban upon two consecutive terms seems unrealistic.

Constitutional qualifications are the same for governor and the other five officers. Each must be at least twenty-five years of age, citizen of the United States for ten years and of Arizona for five years immediately preceding election, a qualified voter of the state, and proficient in the use of the English language. The attorney general is required by statute to have been eligible for practice before the state Supreme Court during the five-year period immediately before his election. Since most Arizona residents, if they live long enough, are able to meet constitutional requirements, other qualifications, such as political skill and experience, are of at least equal importance.

Aside from resignation, death, or defeat at the polls, the governor and other executive officials may be removed from office by the democratic process of recall or the legislative process of impeachment, with the latter being limited to cases involving "high crimes, misdemeanors, or malfeasance in office. . . . " None has been removed by any method. By statute, the legislature has ruled that a vacancy exists in an office when the incumbent has been found guilty of a felony or adjudged insane, or when he has been absent from the state for more than three months without legislative permission, or fails to perform the duties of his office for a period of more than three consecutive months.

In the event of the death, resignation, removal from office, or permanent disability of the governor, the secretary of state, if holding office by election, becomes governor, both in fact and in name. Next in line of succession are the attorney general, state auditor, state treasurer, and superintendent of public instruction.

The governor is by implication the chief executive, although the constitution nowhere uses the title. As chief executive, he has the nominal responsibility for seeing that laws are administered or enforced, exercising some legislative leadership, performing certain judicial functions, and serving as the social and ceremonial head of state government.

In his capacity as chief administrator, the governor "shall transact all executive business with the officers of the government, civil and military, and may require information in writing from the officers in the Executive Department upon any subject relating to the duties of their respective offices" and "he shall take care that the laws be faithfully executed." The governor furthermore is directed by law to supervise the official conduct of all executives and ministerial officials, and he is vested with the authority to require any officer or board to make a special report to him. He has some opportunity to influence administration through his appointive power, as he names more than 200 persons to boards, commissions, and other agencies. Senatorial confirmation usually is required. His removal power is much nar-

46

rower than his appointive power, in cases of appointments for definite terms. He has a fairly free hand, however, in removing officers whom he has appointed for indefinite terms.

In recent years the office of governor has shown some slight tendency to develop into an important center of legislative leadership. The growth of state government as a positive force in the economic and social life of Arizona has contributed to the need for legislative leadership which has not always been met from within the legislature. There is some inclination, moreover, for the people of Arizona to look to the governor for leadership because he, in contrast to members of the legislature, is elected by the voters of the entire state.

The governor has the opportunity to submit a legislative program to the legislative, and to the state at large, when he obeys the constitutional mandate "to communicate, by message, to the legislature at every session the condition of the state, and recommend such matters as he shall deem expedient." He may veto bills passed by the legislature, which in turn may repass them by a two-thirds majority or, if the bills are emergency measures, three-fourths. In addition, he may veto items of appropriation laws. The governor may call the legislature into special session; and the legislature can consider only the proposals listed by the governor in his call. The governor may supplement his constitutional powers for influencing policy-making by bidding for public support for his program, or special measures through press conferences and radio and TV addresses and from the public platform. He may use his influence as a party leader, when his party also controls the legislature, and he may employ persuasion and cajolery in informal conferences with legislative leaders.

In his capacity as social and ceremonial head of the state, the governor welcomes distinguished visitors, makes numerous public addresses and appearances, proclaims special days and weeks, and officiates at dedication ceremonies for public works. Judicial powers of the governor include the granting of reprieves, commutations, and pardons, subject to rules laid down by the legislature, except where treason or impeachment is involved.

The governor of Arizona is essentially a weak chief executive in comparison to the President or to the governors of states which have undergone extensive administrative reorganizations. The constitution disperses executive power among six elective executives, and the governor has little control over the other executives who as elected officers are primarily answerable to the voters. He does not have effective supervisory authority over the numerous boards and commissions, many of whose members have been appointed by his predecessors in office. Even if his administrative authority were greater, he would have great difficulty in directing and coordinating the activities of the executive branch because of the presence of more than 100 separate administrative structures, his virtual lack of a staff, the absence of definite lines of control and responsibility to the nonexistence of service-wide management agencies.

The present position of the governor is attributable to a number of factors ranging from theory to accident. The constitution undoubtedly embodies the twin theories that executive power is a necessary evil and ought to be dispersed in the interest of safety, and that there is a definite relation between democracy and the number of elective, executive offices. Accident probably entered the picture in the unplanned growth of administrative agencies.

The primary responsibility for making laws is vested in the state legislature. Like all but one of its counterparts in other states, the Arizona legislature is bicameral, consisting of the House of Representatives and the Senate. The membership is apportioned among the counties of the state on the basis of the votes cast in the previous election for governor, with each county having at least one. To provide for changes in population, reapportionment of representation among counties is required every four years.

Until 1955 the Senate also reflected population differences with five counties having two senators and others only one. In that year, however, the people approved a constitutional amendment giving to each county two senators, making twenty-eight in all. There are no differences in the qualifications for membership in the House and the Senate, each requiring citizenship, minimum age of twenty-five years, residence of three years in Arizona, residence of one year in the county from which elected, and ability to read and write English. The terms of office for both Senate and House are two years.

There is occasional criticism of the existing system of representation, coming particularly from urban areas, on the ground that the Senate gives an inordinate share of political power to rural areas with a small fraction of the population. The system is defended as necessary to protect the minority interests against overwhelming numbers located in the urban communities. Occasionally there are suggestions, such as that made by the AFL-

CIO in 1959, that a unicameral system be adopted. Such an alteration would require a constituional amendment and appears unlikely to meet with approval.

Membership in the state legislature is not considered a full-time occupation. The legislature met biannually before 1950, but in that year a constitutional amendment was adopted providing for annual sessions. It is necessary, therefore, that the members have some other source of income to supplement their legislative salaries. The members of the present legislature are drawn chiefly from the ranks of businesses of varying kinds, with a liberal admixture of people from farming, ranching, trades, professionals, and retired ranks.

The powers of the legislature are very broad, generally subtitled under what are known as the "police powers" — the power to protect the health, welfare, safety, and morals of the community. The state constitution prohibits the passage of special or local laws relating to the granting of divorce, location of county seats, granting of special privileges to corporations, and numerous other matters. The Declaration of Rights, which is comparable to the Bill of Rights in the Federal Constitution, also limits the legislature. Other limitations relate to imposition of property taxes on widows and veterans, and payment of additional compensation to public employees and private contractors.

It is to be noted that when Bruce Babbitt took over the reins of the Governor's chair on March 4, 1978, the historic role of the governorship up to that time, drastically changed. He elevated the office to new heights throughout his almost nine year tenure which ended in 1986. He altered Arizona's balance of power, restoring to the executive branch co-equal authority and power with the legislative branch. He made it a power wielding benchmark of leadership for all future chief executives.

CHAPTER 9.

Arizona's Fifteen Counties

"We rode the big cavalry horses over the sands of the Maricopa desert, swung in our hammocks under the ramadas; swam in the red waters of the Verde River, ate canned peaches, pink butter and commissary hams, listened for the scratching of the centipedes as they scampered around the edges of our canvas-covered floor, found scorpions in our slippers, and rattlesnakes under our beds."

Martha Summerhays
wife of an Army officer,
Camp McDowell, Arizona, 1865

Arizona has fifteen counties. Herein is a short history of each one. The history of the State of Arizona is very much a part of the history of these counties. Unlike counties in many other states, each county in Arizona is so rich with its folklore and culture, that each could be a history book in itself. Only three of the counties have non Indian names.

APACHE COUNTY: Apache County was created out of the eastern two-fifths of Yavapai County on February 24, 1879. Before this division Yavapai County included, roughly, the northern half of that part of the State which lies east of Yuma and Mohave Counties. In 1881 part of the southern Apache County between the Black and Gila Rivers was cut off to form part of Graham County and later, in 1895, the remainder of Apache County was nearly halved, and the western portion became Navajo County. Apache County's present area is 7,151,360 acres. Snowflake was designated the county seat when it was first formed. After the first elections in the fall of 1879, the county government was set up at St. Johns. In 1880 St. Johns was superseded by Springerville. Springerville remained the county seat for only two years until 1882, when St. Johns again became the county seat and has remained so to the present time.

Apache County was named for the Indians of Arizona and New Mexico. Apache Indians did not exist as a single group or nation, but the term had been adopted as applying comprehensively to many tribes known for their warlike characteristics. Even the Navajos were considered Apaches as late at 1800.

Cattle raising and farming were the main sources of livelihood for the earliest settlers in what is now Apache County. In the early 1900's lumbering operations were begun in the White Mountains. Though many family farms are still operating in Apache County, most of the economic activity in that part of the county which is not set aside for the Navajo Reservation is based on tourism, livestock, and forest products. The reservation area of the county depends heavily on Federal Bureau of Indian Affairs activities, sheep raising, and some logging. Tourism to Canyon de Chelly promises to become more important as roads are improved. Oil and gas exploration in the Four Corners area and the helium extraction plant in the Pinta Dome site have improved the economic outlook for Apache County. The earliest known non-Indian settlement in Apache County was the Mexican community of Concho, established in the late 1860's and still in existence. The community was taken over in 1879 by Mormon settlers who called the town Erastus for a short time, but returned to the name Concho in 1890.

The next known settlement which is still an active community today is Springerville. In 1875 Harry Springer established a store, bringing merchandise from Albuquerque. The place was known than as Springer's Store. Springer made the mistake of trusting outlaws with feed and seed and soon went broke. The townspeople jokingly called their town Springerville after he left, and that was the name given to the post office when it was established in 1879.

Shortly after Springer's failure and departure, Julius and Gustav Becker established a store in the same area in August of 1876. The Beckers used ox trains to bring in supplies until 1890, when they changed to horses and mules. After 1895 a branch railroad was completed to Magdalena, New Mexico, to speed transportation. The Becker Store is still the main store in Springerville. A son of Gustav Becker helped to establish the first transcontinental highway. The first automobile to make the coast-to-coast trip was driven through Springerville in 1910. Springerville attracts many summer visitors due to its cool climate, recreational facilities, and good hunting and fishing.

St. Johns, at the site of an early Little Colorado River crossing, was first called El Vadito by Spanish explorers. In 1873 Solomon Barth, an Indian trader, won cattle and land in a poker game played with Mexicans who had settled at the crossing, and he remained there with his brothers Nathan and Morris. He changed the name from El Vadito to San Juan (Spanish for St. John). Other white men had established cattle ranches near San Juan and the name was Americanized to St. Johns sometime before 1879, when it first became the county seat. In 1875 Solomon Barth sold his interests to a Mormon agent, but the Mormons did not start a community there until 1880. This community was called Salem and was a mile north of St. Johns. It was abandoned about six months later when the Mormons moved into St. Johns. This move assured the continuation of that settlement.

Another early town in Apache County which is still active today is Eager, which was established in 1888 on ground given to the town by John, Joel, and William Eager, who had homesteaded in Round Valley in 1878. Eagar was the site of an outlaw battle in which nine members of the Snider Gang were killed. The exact date of the fracas is in doubt, but it probably took place prior to 1900.

McNary was originally called Cluff Cienega after a Mormom Bishop named Cluff. It gradually grew into a sawmill town as the lumbering industry developed in the White Mountains during the early 1900's. The lumber company called the town Cooley in honor of Corydon E. Cooley, a famous Indian scout under General Crook. When the McNary Lumber Company bought the property in 1924, the name was changed to McNary.

Principal Industries: lumbering, tourism, livestock, forest products.

Points of Interest: Petrified National Forest, Painted Desert, Canyon de Chelly, Monument Valley, Four Corners, Window Rock, Navajo Tribal Headquarters.

Recreation Area: Big and Crescent Lakes, Apache Reservation, Sunrise Ski Lodge, McNary and Eager Wood Products, Concho Country Club.

County Seat: St. Johns.

Elevation: 5,650 feet.

COCHISE COUNTY: Cochise County, named for Cochise, the famous leader of the Chiricahua Apache Indians, came into existence on February 1, 1881. Its area was originally the southeastern corner of Pima County. Tombstone was the original county seat and remained so until 1929 when the county offices were moved to Bisbee, which had become far more active and prosperous. The present area of the County is 4,003,840 acres —

as large an area as the states of Connecticut and Rhode Island together.

The first census figure pertaining to what is now Cochise County was for Apache Pass in 1870. This was a very strategic settlement as it was on the only trail through the Chiricahua Mountains, the main Apache stronghold in Arizona. The Butterfield Overland Stage established a station at Apache Pass in 1857 to provide protection for its passengers. The pass formed a perfect ambush spot, and Apaches slaughtered passengers of stagecoaches and whole wagon trains without danger to themselves. Early in 1858 President Butterfield asked the Federal Government to establish a fort, but he suspended operations in Southern Arizona before Fort Bowie was established in 1862. The official post office name was not changed from Apache Pass to Fort Bowie until 1880. The fort has since been abandoned, and the land was sold at public auction in 1911.

Gold and silver at Tombstone and copper at Bisbee were discovered in the same year — 1877 — but copper ore was so much more difficult to process that most of the early development occurred at Tombstone. The present Willcox area was the next to be developed when the coming of the railroad provided an opportunity to establish a shipping center for cattle. The economic history of Cochise County has been closely tied to the fortunes of the copper mining industry and the military establishment at Fort Huachuca. In recent years agriculture has become economically important, with many diversified crops being grown; and cattle raising has become continually important. The future looks bright for the county with recent expansion of the Lavender Pit Mine, the construction and operaton of the Electronic Environmental Test Corridor, and industrial growth in Douglas and Willcox.

Tombstone first appeared in the Census of 1880 with a population of 973. The fame of the rich silver and gold discoveries drew thousands of people, including a goodly number of outlaws. Between 1880 and 1890 the town grew to a reputed fifteen thousand population — larger than San Francisco — and was considered the most cultured city in the entire Southwest. The most famous musicians and actors of the world played at the Bird Cage Theatre during these few years. In 1888 the mines began flooding and the town withered rapidly. Its population had dropped to less than two thousand by 1890, and it was virtually a ghost town until recent years. Tombstone is now a world renowned attraction for tourists who come to see the locale of famous outlaw battles, Boothill Cemetery, and the Bird Cage Theatre Museum. It also houses many who work at Fort Huachuca. Recent oil exploration shows promise and might possibly bring another boom to Tombstone.

Bisbee was founded on the mining of copper rather than the more precious metals and, due to the more difficult extraction processes, did not attract the sudden rush of get-rich-quick people as did Tombstone. However, when Bisbee did start to grow as capital for mine development became available, its economic base proved to be more stable than Tombstone's. Original financial backing came from Judge Bisbee of San Francisco, although he never visited the town named for him. In 1881 the Phelps Dodge Company, represented by Dr. James Douglas, staked and developed claims adjoining the original Copper Queen claims. The two companies merged in 1885, making greater development and expansion possible. In spite of labor troubles, two world wars, and ensuing depressions, Bisbee has hung on as an established city due to expert long-range planning and development by the copper companies. It started losing population immediately after the stock market crash in 1929 and dwindled from over nine thousand in 1920 to less than four thousand in 1950. During the 1940's Bisbee was plagued with a shortage of skilled labor, and this persisted even after World War II. Conversion to open-pit mining took several years, up to 1951, when the Lavender Pit Mine was opened; and the Bisbee area population more than tripled by 1960.

Douglas was assured of permanency when the Copper Queen Mining Company build a smelter there in 1901, and a public utilities corporation was formed in 1902. The town was named for Dr. James Douglas, who had given technical advice on the construction of the smelter. Douglas grew rapidly until 1920 and has been fairly stable since that time. Copper smelting is still the largest industry in Douglas, but a few small factories add to the economy. The major agricultural crop is chiles which are processed in a small seasonal cannery.

Willcox was originally called Maley because the railroad which caused it to exist was built through the ranch of a man named Maley. The name was changed to Willcox almost immediately when General Orlando B. Willcox, Commander of the Department of Arizona, came through the town on the train in 1880. The town was built as a cattle shipping center and a trading center for the surrounding cattle ranches. More recently, irrigated acreage has been developed to grow lettuce, cotton, and other cash crops. In addition, small grains are grown for pen feeding cattle.

Fort Huachuca was established in 1877 and was of great importance as a military post until the surrender of Geronimo in 1886. The fort was relatively inactive until 1911, when it became headquarters for troops posted along the Mexican border to protect Arizona against raids during a Mexican revolt. It reached maximum importance during World War II when twenty-two thousand military and eight thousand civilians were stationed there. Since World War II it has been activated and deactivated several times, but became an electronic proving ground in the early 1950's and has every prospect of remaining a permanent and extremely important military establishment. Sierra Vista has grown around Fort Huachuca to provide off-post housing for civilian personnel. The military and civilian payrolls, as well as the expenditures for supplies, are of tremendous importance to the economy of Cochise County and the whole State.

The County Seat is Bisbee and its elevation is 5,350 feet.

COCONINO COUNTY: Coconino County was formed out of the northwestern corner of Yavapai County on February 19, 1891. It was named for the Coconino Indians. The county, having an area of 11,886,720 acres, is the largest county in Arizona and the second largest in the United States. The county is most famous for the scenic wonder of the Grand Canyon. Only about one-third of the county is privately owned land. Nearly one-third of the total area is Navajo, Hopi, Hualapai, and Kaibab Indian reservation land. Another third is taken up by the Kaibab and Coconino National Forests and national parks and monuments, the largest of which is the Grand Canyon National Park. The highest mountain is Humphrey's Peak (12,670 feet) in Coconino County. Flagstaff is the county seat.

The earliest settlements in what is now Coconino County were devoted primarily to cattle ranching, though Mormons attempted to start an agricultural settlement around 1873 at the site of the present Tuba City. Five years later the Mormon leader, Erastus Snow, laid out the present town site of Tuba City, and Mormons settled there to farm, not realizing that it was on Navajo reservation land. At about the same time, Mormons also attempted to start woolen mills at what is now Moenkopi. They expected that the Indians would furnish their labor supply, but the project was soon abandoned.

William Bass capitalized on the tourist value of the Grand Canyon when he discovered an Indian train into the Canyon and set up tent houses for guests. Bass also mined copper and asbestos and, when a branch railroad line was built to handle his ores, it brought tourists in large numbers. Tourism has remained a major economic factor. The construction of Glen Canyon Dam began in 1957 in the northeastern corner of the county. It has had, and will continue to have an important economic impact on the county. For a long time lumbering has been the chief industry of the county, as the area has an abundance of commercial grade trees.

The city of Page was established shortly after construction began on the Glen Canyon Dam in 1957 to house construction and government workers and their families. It has grown into a fair-sized community. Page was named for John Chatfield Page, Commissioner of Reclaimation, 1937 to 1953.

Williams is the only early settlement besides Flagstaff that has maintained status as an incorporated city in Coconino County. The first two white men settled there in 1876 but sold out their interests the next year. The post office was established in June, 1881, and the coming of the railroad started Williams on its long history of prosperity to poverty to prosperity. It gradually became an important lumbering and railroad town and is known today as the "Gateway to the Grand Canyon."

GILA COUNTY: Gila County was formed from portions of Maricopa and Pinal Counties on February 8, 1881. Its area was extended eastward to the San Carlos River by petition in 1889. Part of its southern boundary is the Gila River, for which the county was named. It contains 3,040,000 acres, making it nearly equal in size to Graham County. The county seat was established at Globe and has remained there. More than one-half of the area in Gila County is occupied by the San Carlos Indian Reservation, and almost all the rest of it is taken up by the Tonto National Forest. The only privately owned lands in the whole county are a small rectangle surrounding the Globe-Miami district, and a slightly larger area in the triangle formed by the southern boundary. The Federal Government controls ninety-four per cent of the land in the county.

Mining and livestock raising are the principal industries of Gila County. This will continue to be true, although the completion of State Highway 65, from Phoenix and over the Mogollon Rim, has made the Tonto Basin-Payson recreational area easily accessible to Salt River Valley residents. Many have summer homes in the area and a great many more drive up for weekend hunting, fishing, and camping.

Mining is the most important industry. The Inspiration Consolidated Copper Company and the Miami Copper Company have mines and smelters working near Globe and Miami, and construction of a complete mill and development of the mine at Christmas is going forward. There are three new asbestos mills in operation which, it is hoped, will attract manufacturers of asbestos products.

The oldest and most important community in Gila County is Globe. Globe grew into a community in 1875 after the first discovery of rich silver ores in the district had taken place in 1874. These discoveries were soon worked out, and Globe might have relapsed into oblivion if the Silver King Mine, twenty miles southwest, and the Stonewall Jackson Mine, twenty miles northwest, had not been discovered in 1875. Both of these were very rich and extensive locations. Globe was in a strategic place to benefit from both, as it already had a smelter built and had a good water supply. There was an immediate stampede of bonanza hunters creating the towns of Pinal City at the Silver King (population of 166 in the 1880 census), and McMillanville at the Stonewall Jackson Mine (population of 150 in the 1880 census). Pinal City was on the site of the Southwest Arboretum; no traces of it can be found today. McMillanville has two adobe shacks in very poor condition still standing among rusted pieces of roofing, mining machinery, and faint outlines of foundations. The silver in the mines was worked out by 1885, and both towns were deserted by 1890. Globe, however, continued to grow because rich copper deposits were found there in early 1880's. The development of the copper mines in the area expanded smelter operations and created the town of Miami in 1907. The Inspiration Mine Company constructed a huge reduction plant there in 1909 which has led to Miami sometimes being called the "Concentrator City."

Although Globe is one of the State's oldest incorporated cities, it has not been incorporated continuously. It first incorporated in 1880. Sometime during the next twenty-five years the townspeople apparently forgot it was incorporated, for in 1905 they did it again. This time, citizens of Globe decided it was too expensive and disbanded their Articles of Incorporation. Finally, they incorporated once more in 1907 and have remained an incorporated city since.

Central Heights is a residential suburb of Globe, although not within the city limits. It was originally an area of mine owners' residences, closer to the mines than to the town and smelter.

Hayden was started in 1910 as a mill and smelter town for the mines in the southern tip of the county.

Winkelman is a shipping point for cattle for the various ranches in the valleys surrounding the junction of the Gila and San Pedro Rivers. It is expected to expand considerably when the mine at Christmas gets into operation.

Principal Industries: mining, livestock, tourism.

Points of Interest: Salt River Canyon, Tonto National Monument, Coolidge Dam, Roosevelt Dam, Kinishba Ruins.

County Seat: Globe.

Elevation: 3,540 feet.

GRAHAM COUNTY: Graham County was created on March 10, 1881, from parts of Apache and Pima Counties. It is assumed that the county was named for Graham Mountain. Isadore Solomon started the county seat in his sawmill which was known as Solomonville; but, shortly afterward, the county seat was moved to Safford. It stayed there until 1883, when it was returned to Solomonville. After Greenlee County was split from Graham County in 1911, the county seat moved back to Safford, where it has remained. The present Graham County has an area of 2,950,400 acres. There are three portions of the Coronado National Forest in Graham County, and approximately one-third of the county area is Indian reservation land.

Graham County started as an agricultural area, and agriculture has remained its primary economic base. Copper and lead mining have varied in importance to the county and are presently at a low level. However, some exploration is being conducted in the Safford area. Tourism is of importance, particularly in mountain resorts during the summer months.

A new Camp Grant was established in what is now Graham County when the unhealthy location of old Camp Grant in Pinal County and its unsavory reputation due to the massacre of Aravaipa Indians there in 1871, caused the military to seek a more suitable location. The shift was accomplished either in late 1872 or in early 1873, and troops were shifted to the new Camp Grant from Camp Crittenden (in Santa Cruz County) as well as from old Camp Grant. The only census figure ever recorded for Camp Grant was 243 in 1880. The name was changed to Fort Grant in 1879, but the establishment was already losing its importance as Fort Huachuca became the major post in Southern Arizona. The possible time. The average rainfall is 7.2 inches a year. Much of the county is used for agriculture, depending on a vast network of irrigation canals from the dammed Salt and Verde Rivers.

The primary cities in the county are Phoenix, Scottsdale, Tempe, Mesa, Glendale, and Chandler. About eight-five percent of the county's population and forty-seven percent of the State's population is contained within these coterminous areas. The airline service is provided by three transcontinental and six regional carriers providing both passenger and air freight service with approximately one hundred scheduled arrivals and departures daily from the Phoenix area. The Santa Fe and Southern Pacific Railroads offer railway connections for freight and, to a limited extent, passenger travel. The county is served by two national bus lines along transcontinental routes. There is one main bus line operating within the metropolitan area of Phoenix. The outer portion of the central urbanized section of the county is served by another bus line which offers only service between the suburbs but not within the suburbs. Because of the geographic dispersion of major industry and wide location of workers, public transportation is inadequate. For those with their own transportation, there are over twenty-six miles of completed freeway within Phoenix linking the city with uninterrupted freeway travel from Flagstaff to Tucson (Interstate 10 and Interstate 17). The excellent highways through the county are a major factor in the county's becoming a regional warehousing and distribution center. These highways are main arteries vital to the warehousing and distribution firms. The area is serviced by ten transcontinental truck lines, four transcontinental heavy equipment haulers, and three transcontinental automobile transporters. There are thirty interstate truck lines, thirty-nine intra-state truck lines, also REA Express and United Parcel Service.

More than one thousand years prior to the coming of the white man, the ancient Hohokam Indians were diverting waters from the Salt and Gila Rivers and cultivating the fertile river valleys. Settlement of what is now Phoenix began in 1865, when a hay supply point for Camp McDowell was set up about four miles from the present center of Phoenix. Prior to World War II, agriculture, tourism, government and some food and fiber processing, stimulated by availability of irrigation water in the Salt River Valley, were the principal factors influencing growth in Maricopa County. During World War II, the U.S. Government encouraged the establishment of a number of basic industries in the Valley. After the war, the production was maintained, and in 1956 the

fort was abandoned in 1905, and in 1912 the State of Arizona took over the old fort.

Safford was the next settlement in what is now Graham County. In 1874 a group of farmers who had been living in Gila Bend and whose land was periodically washed out by the flooding Gila River followed the river to find a better location and settled the first American colony of civilians in the Gila Valley at Safford. The first store was established by Joshua Bailey during 1874, and the post office was established in March, 1875, in the store. Safford has remained primarily a farming community, though some copper and lead mining have developed; and exploration of copper claims north of Safford is in progress now. Tourism has become fairly important in and around Safford, and the city has drawn numerous retired workers for permanent residence in the past few years. It has grown from a population of 173 in 1880 to nearly five thousand in 1960.

Camp Thomas was established in 1876 in the Gila River Valley to replace old Camp Goodwin where malaria was quite prevalent. It was located about twenty miles northwest of Safford and only about six miles east of the old Camp Goodwin. The camp developed slowly and was built by the soldiers themselves because the Government, stung by the expensive abandonment of Camp Goodwin, would not provide funds. The name was changed to Fort Thomas in 1883. Funds finally became available in 1884 and a handsome post was built, but the surrender of Geronimo in 1886 reduced the need for the fort and it was abandoned in 1892. Fort Thomas is still an active community, but it has never incorporated and has remained fairly small.

The present town of Pima was originally settled by Mormons in 1879 and was named Smithville after the Mormon leader, President Jesse N. Smith. Malaria and outlaws caused many problems, but the residents preserved and maintained the community. The name was changed to Pima when the post office was established in August, 1880. Pima incorporated before 1940 and has been listed in each census since 1890. It is still active community but has been losing population gradually since 1930.

Thatcher is another community which was settled by Mormons about 1882. The first town site was selected in 1883, but it was relocated on higher ground two years later. The name was chosen after a visit by the Mormon Apostle, Moses Thatcher. The post office was not established until 1888. Thatcher was, as most Mormon settlements are, an agricultural community and has remained essentially that, although Eastern Arizona Junior College was established there in 1891. Thatcher grew rapidly in population through 1910 and has grown gradually since.

Principal Industries: agriculture, livestock.

Points of Interest: Mt. Graham, San Carlos Lake, Aravaipa Canyon, Fort Grant, San Carlos Indian Reservation.

County Seat: Safford.

Elevation: 2,900 feet.

GREENLEE COUNTY: Greenlee County was created in 1911 from the eastern part of Graham County. The county was legally created by an Act of the Twenty-fifth Arizona Territorial Legislature on March 10, 1909, but political difficulties between the parent county and the new county, delayed organization of Greenlee into an active county until 1911. The county contains 1,199,360 acres and more than half of the county area is included in the Apache and Gila National Forests. The division between Graham and Greenlee Counties was made along the same boundary line as the eastern boundary of the San Carlos Indian Reservation. The county seat is at Clifton, the oldest community. The county was named after Mason Greenlee, an early settler who made the first location in the Greenlee mining district near Clifton. He first came to the area in 1874, but was forced by Indians to leave. He returned in 1879 and stayed the rest of his life.

The early development of Greenlee County was due to mining, which is still extremely important in this area. Cattle raising is also a main industry, although copper production has increased since 1950 and the production of molybdenum has reached significant proportions since that time. Modernization of methods has reduced the number of employed in the mining industry.

Clifton began as a community in 1872 when a group of prospectors, including Charles Shannon, the Lezinsky brothers, and two others named Metcalf and Stevens, explored the area and established copper mines. Exceedingly rich ore had been discovered there by an army scout in 1869, but he was not able to develop it. It is believed that the town was named because of its location in the midst of towering cliffs, although there was an early-day prospector named Henry Clifton who traveled through the district prior to 1872. Backed by Eastern capital, the Detroit Copper Company was organized to develop the claims at Clifton. Copper claims were located on Copper Mountain, the present site of Morenci, as early as 1881. The mining town was known as Joy's Camp at that time. It was changed to Morenci in 1882 when the Detroit Copper Company bought the claims and built the smelter there. Arizona's first copper concentrator was built at Morenci in 1886.

The coming of the railroad into the area was a great boon to development. In 1883 the railroad was completed and Duncan was established as the railroad shipping point for mining in the Clifton-Morenci area, as well as a cattle shipping point for ranches in what is now Greenlee County.

Metcalf was the mining town for the Metcalf mining claims which were close enough to Clifton to use the smelter there. By 1915 the ores in the Metcalf area had played out and the town gradually died away. The depression following World War I and the depletion of high-grade ore in both Clifton and Morenci, brought hard times to the area and many moved away during the 1920's.

Though the town of Morenci shows a sixty-three percent loss in population since 1950, the actual loss for the area was only 1,483 or twenty-nine percent, as many Morenci residents merely moved to new housing constructed by Phelps Dodge Corporation in nearby areas listed as Plantsite and Stargo in the 1960 census. This population shift made possible the razing of the old houses in order to get at ore, which though worthless at the time Morenci was built, had become valuable due to the introduction of new mining and processing methods. Another factor in this loss of population in the Morenci area is the trend toward commuting. Many miners are settling their families in Safford and even in Lordsburg, New Mexico, and commuting to work in Morenci.

Principal Industries: mining, livestock.

Points of Interest: Coronado Trail, Hannagan Meadows, Blue River, Morenci open pit mines.

County Seat: Clifton.

Elevation: 3,465 feet.

MARICOPA COUNTY: Maricopa County, lying in the south-central part of Arizona, covers an area of 9,253 square miles of desert valley and low mountain ranges. The Tonto National Forest, with its 7,645-foot Four Peaks Mountain, the desert region in the southwest portion of the county, and the 1,300 miles of canals which criss-cross the county's central portion, all contribute to the topographical diversity characterizing the county. It encompasses three Indian reservations — Salt River, Fort McDowell, Gila Bend — and a small part of the Gila River Reservation. The average temperature range is between 75 degrees and 104.6 degrees in summer and between 35 degrees and 64 degrees in winter, with the sun shining eighty-eight percent of the

value of industrial output for the state exceeded the value of agricultural products. Industrial development has kept pace with the vigorous population increase, with manufacturing showing the greatest increase.

Agriculture has historically been a major component of the county's economic base, with the county currently encompassing forty-four per cent of the state's cultivated crop land. Maricopa County is the state's largest single county producer in all major crop categories. The chief crops are cotton, alfalfa, cereal grains, lettuce, onions, and sugar beets. The county is the third most important county in the U.S. in terms of agricultural output. At the same time, however, agricultural employment has been slowly declining since 1950, due to increased mechanization and consolidation of farms into larger, more efficient operations.

The tourist industry, which includes the services industry, is a major contributor to the county economy. Natural and manmade attractions in the area, together with the climate, have made the Valley a prime vacation spot for the state and nation.

The trade section of the economy is the largest employer in the Valley. The improvement of interstate highway transportation through the Valley, as well as the central location of Phoenix within the thirteen-state and Northern Mexico market, have made the county a wholesale and retail distribution center. Population growth has been the major stimulus to the growth of the government sector. Government is the third largest employer including state, local, and federal employees, many of whom are involved with education.

Principal Industries: agriculture, light industry, tourism, government business, electronics and high tech.

Points of Interest: Phoenix Art Museum, Heard Museum, Phoenix Zoo, Pueblo Grande prehistoric ruins, Arizona State University, Apache Trail, Arizona Temple, Desert Botanical Gardens.

County Seat: Phoenix.

Elevation: 1,117 feet.   Population: About 2 million

MOHAVE COUNTY: Mohave County is the second largest county in Arizona. Its total area encompasses 13,403 square miles of which 176 square miles is covered by water, supplying the county with an estimated one thousand miles of shoreline on navigable rivers and lakes. The county is bordered on the north and the west by the states of California, Nevada, and Utah; and three lakes, Havasu, Mohave, and Mead, help make up the western borders along the Colorado River. Elevation ranges from five hundred to eight thousand feet, with most of the terrain classified as desert. The higher areas of the county, however, are covered by vegetation types, characterized as scrub oak and pinon pine and Ponderosa pine in the higher levels.

The climate of Mohave County is generally arid. Kingman, at an elevation of 3,345 feet, has an average maximum temperature of seventy-six degrees and an annual minimum temperature of forty-six degrees. Humidity is low, and precipitation averages about eleven inches annually. The higher elevations of the county receive snow in the winter, and all of Mohave County, like most of Arizona, is subject to wide climatic extremes. In Kingman, for example, the lowest daily minimum temperature occurs in January (31 degrees) and the highest daily average is in July (98 degrees).

Kingman, the county seat, is the largest city in the county. Lake Havasu City and Bullhead City, the other majors towns, are located on the Colorado River. Both freight and passenger service on the Santa Fe Railroad are available at Kingman. Bus transportation is furnished by Greyhound, Continental Trailways, and the Las Vegas-Tonapah-Reno Stage. Regular airline service is maintained from Kingman and Lake Havasu City by scheduled flights to Phoenix, Las Vegas, and Los Angeles. Local, intrastate and interstate trucking service is available.

Historically, mining has formed the major base of Mohave County's economy. Mining towns rose virtually overnight and waned just as quickly as deposits of gold and silver were discovered and depleted. In the early 1960's, there began an interest in the copper-molybdenum deposits in the area. The Duval Corporation operates an open-pit mine at Ithaca Peak, north of Kingman. The Standard Copper Company is developing the Copper World Mine, an underground operation near Yucca, south of Kingman. The El Paso Mine has been completed and is in full operation as an open-pit mine. Nonmetallic mining is being conducted to extract sand and gravel, stone and feldspar deposits.

The major agricultural pursuit in the county is the production of beef cattle. Sheep raising is also conducted, although on a much smaller scale. Crop production is limited, consisting primarily of feeder crops, especially alfalfa.

The manufacturing industry is a relatively new influence on the county's economy. McCulloch Corporation opened the first production facility in Lake Havasu City and has announced plans to concentrate future expansion in that area. Ford Motor Company established an automotive proving ground near Yucca, Arizona, and also anticipates expansion. The Midwest Wax Paper Company has established operations at the Kingman Airport.

In terms of employment, the largest section in Mohave County is government, followed by trades and services, in support of a growing tourist industry.

The outlook for Mohave County is generally one of continued growth with the growth at Lake Havasu City leading the way. Several new manufacturing plants are currently scheduled for Havasu City, and the services industry should continue to grow with the rapid increase in population.

The Kingman area should grow tremendously. Tourism, Kingman's primary industry, could increase as the area becomes better known.

Bullhead City and its surrounding area should continue to grow. A large segment of Bullhead City's growth must be credited to part-time residents who establish houses and trailers along the Colorado River as recreational and holiday dwellings. Services is the primary industry, and this should grow as the area develops.

Principal Industries: mining, livestock, manufacturing, tourism.

Points of Interest: Colorado River, Lake Havasu, Hualapai Indian Reservation, Davis Dam, Hoover Dam, Grand Canyon National Monument.
County Seat: Kingman.
Elevation: 3,345 feet.

NAVAJO COUNTY: Navajo County, fifth largest county in Arizona, is located in the northeastern part of the state adjacent to the Utah state boundary. Navajo County's 9,915 square miles extend in a fifty-mile wide stretch for approximately 225 miles. The Navajo, Hopi, and Apache Indian Reservations constitute a large portion of the land area of the county. The Mogollon Rim divides the county into two distinct physiographic areas, the Colorado Plateau and a rugged mountainous area. The high plateau country in the northern part of Navajo County is arid and desert-like, abounding with mesas and smaller plateaus. The southern part of the county is a rugged mountainous area, heavily wooded with pinon, juniper, and Ponderosa pine.

The climate of the region has extremes from limited rainfall in the northern half to heavy precipitation in the form of rain and snow in the southern mountain regions.

Approximately one-third of Navajo County's population is located in a strip that is traversed by the Santa Fe Railway and U.S. Highway 66 (Interstate 40). This strip lies just below the Navajo and Hopi Reservations and contains Winslow, the largest city in the county, and Holbrook, the second largest city and the county seat. Other sizeable communities in Navajo County include Show Low, Snowflake, Pinetop, and Heber-Overgaard. There are also several smaller trading centers on the Indian reservations serving a rather widely dispersed Indian population.

Historically, Navajo County's economy has been based on grazing, forest products, and transportation. During the past decade, however, there has been an increasing trend toward diversification of the county's economic base. The processing of forest products has expanded from primarily logging to include molding and millwork firms and a paper manufacturing plant. A garment manufacturing plant and development of tourist accommodations both on and off the Indian reservations, along with increased construction activity, have also been responsible for much of this diversification.

The current economy of Navajo County is relatively stable, with some seasonal effects due to weather. According to employment figures, the major industrial sectors of the economy are government, services, trade, manufacturing, and transportation. Tourism along U. S. Highway 66 is more extensive during the summer months, and declines during the winter months, causing a subsequent decline in the services and trade industries. Manufacturing also exhibits a decline in employment during the winter months. This is because much of Navajo County's manufacturing, centered around wood products and logging activities which supply the mills with raw material, comes to a halt during the winters. There is also some seasonal employment in highway and railway maintenance, with substantial increases in the summer months.

Government employees are mostly federal, with the major agency employers being the U. S. Public Health Service, the Bureau of Indian Affairs, and the U. S. Forest Service.

Principal Industries: lumbering, agriculture, livestock, Indian crafts and trading, tourism.

Points of Interest: Petrified Forest National Park, Painted Desert, White Mountains, Hopi Indian Villages, Navajo National Monument, Monument Valley.

County Seat: Holbrook.

Elevation: 5,069 feet.

PIMA COUNTY: Pima County is one of the four original counties created by the First Territorial Legislature on November 8, 1864. It was the home of the Pima Indians, a peaceful, agricultural tribe, for whom the county was named. The original county consisted of all Arizona south of the Gila River and east of Yuma County (almost all of the Gadsden Purchase). As the other counties were formed, Pima lost large portions to Maricopa, Pinal, Cochise, Graham, and Santa Cruz; this left Pima with an area of 5,914,240 acres.

A large section of Pima County is occupied by the Papago Indian Reservation. The small San Xavier Indian Reservation is also within its boundaries. It has two national monuments — both cactus forests — the Organ Pipe National Monument and the Saguaro National Monument. The Santa Catalina Mountains, north of Tucson, are a part of Coronado National Forest.

Almost all industries existing in other counties of Arizona are also found in Pima County, with the exception of lumbering. Some lumbering was done in the 1870's in the Santa Rita Mountains, but it was not extensive. Tourism, trade, agriculture, educational developments, modern transportation, and industrial developments are centered in Tucson, while mining is extensive in other parts of the county.

The first known census of Tucson was taken August 6, 1820, giving a population of 384. The earliest recollections of a Tucson resident, born there in 1819, describe it as a Mexican military post of about ninety soldiers, about 140 adobe hovels without doors or framed windows, and a population of about three hundred people who farmed in the valley west of the town and cultivated fruit and vegetables which they sold to the government. The Mexican Government never kept a large enough military establishment at Tucson to keep the Apaches under control, and Tucson could not grow. Even the farmland close to town was not sufficiently free from Apache raids and terror to provide a stable economy. In 1858 mail lines and a stage line were established, but the real growth of the town could not occur until some time after Arizona became a separate territory in 1863. Camp Lowell was established as headquarters of military administration for Southern Arizona, enabling Tucson to become the outfitting and supply point for all trade in Northwestern Mexico as well as Southern and Eastern Arizona. Trade with Sonora expanded rapidly, due to the fact that goods cost but little more delivered at Tucson than by water at Guaymas. At Guaymas the payment of customs and port duties was unavoidable, but goods arriving at Tucson could be packed in 100 to 150-pound packs and sent by mule train to all points in Northern Mexico without payment of any type of taxes or duties. Tucson thus had a monopoly on trade with Sonora; this is the chief reason for its extremely rapid growth between 1866 and about 1900.

In 1861, Tucson, with a total of sixty-eight American voters, elected a delegate to the Confederate Congress; and this action made Arizona County of New Mexico Territory a part of the Confederacy. In June, 1862, however, General Carleton's California Volunteers entered Tucson and officially returned Arizona County to the Union.

Hundreds of thousands of dollars were lost in the Ajo mines from 1861 to 1911 through poor management, lack of knowledge, and deliberate swindles such as bogus reduction methods. In 1911 the Calumet and Arizona Company bought the properties, developed a permanent water supply, and invented processes for leaching the ore. The mine began intensified production in 1917. Ajo was reported in the census for the first time in 1920. In spite of the ups and downs of copper production and prices, Ajo has shown a continuous growth in each census report since.

Principal Industries: mining, defense-oriented manufacturing, agriculture, tourism.

Points of Interest: San Xavier del Bac Mission, Arizona-Sonora Desert Museum, Saguaro National Monument, Colossal Cave and Park, Kitt Peak National Observatory, Organ Pipe Cactus National Monument, University of Arizona.

County Seat: Tucson.

Elevation: 2,410 feet.

PINAL COUNTY: Pinal County was created from parts of Maricopa and Pima Counties on February 1, 1875. At that time it included the rich Globe mining district, but in 1881 this area was lost to Gila County. Its present area is 3,441,920 acres. The origin of the name "Pinal" is lost; it could have been derived from the Pinal Apaches or from the pine groves in the high mountains. The county seat has been established in Florence since the formation of the county. Almost all of the Gila River and the Maricopa Indian Reservations and small portions of the Pima and the San Carlos Reservations are in this county. It also contains a portion of the Tonto National Forest. The history and economics of Pinal County are tied to the Gila River. Even today the river is of great importance for providing water, either directly or indirectly, for the widespread agriculture of the county, as well as being a part of its boundary. Rich agricultural districts throughout the center and rich mining developments in the northern and eastern mountains have characterized the growth of the county. New industries and developments within recent years are providing variety, including such diverse things as a baseball training camp, a steel mill, and a large retirement community.

The earliest recorded settlement in Pinal County was Maricopa Wells with a population of fifty-three, first listed in the Census of 1860. It was important, as early as 1857, as a station on the San Antonio-San Diego mail route, the last place to get water before crossing the "Forty-Mile Desert" to the big bend of the Gila River. It is now the little community of Maricopa on the Maricopa Indian Reservation.

By the Census of 1870 two new towns had sprung up in Pinal County: Adamsville in 1865 and Florence in 1868 (named by Territorial Governor Richard McCormick for his sister). Adamsville was a freighting and trading center on the Gila River, four miles west of Florence. It was the location of a flour mill, the only one between Tucson and California, and supplied many Arizona forts with flour. As Florence grew, Adamsville sank; the flour mill was moved and the town gradually disappeared. Florence developed as the center of the agricultural district of the upper Gila River. It later became a meeting point of stage routes to Prescott, Ehrenberg, Phoenix, Tucson, Yuma, and the rich mining districts of Silver King and Globe. The building of Coolidge Dam and the Ashurst-Hayden Diversion Dam on the Gila provided irrigation for the area, insuring its importance as an agricultural area. The Territorial Prison was transferred from Yuma to Florence in 1909, and it is the site of the State Prison today.

In 1878 an extremely rich silver strike, known as the Silver King, was made in the mountains near present-day Superior. Very shortly, other mines and others towns sprang up in the district, none of which lasted beyond the life of the silver ores which were worked out by 1890. These were Silver King, Pinal City (see the history of Globe in Gila County), Silver Queen, and Reymert. The present town of Superior is at the location known as Silver King in 1880 and Silver Queen in 1882, as the community had no official name distinct from the mines. The town site of Superior was officially laid out in 1900 and named after the Arizona and Lake Superior Mining Company, the owner of the mines at that time. The Silver Queen proved more lasting than the Silver King because large underlying deposits of copper were found after the silver ore played out. On these, the community managed to stay alive until the Magma Copper Company bought the properties in 1910. The Magma Copper Company developed and expanded copper mining in the area and built a large smelter at Superior in 1916, thus insuring its continuance.

Mammoth was the milling town on the San Pedro River set up to serve the old Mammoth Mine which was being worked for gold as early as 1873. The mine continued intermittently until 1901. In 1934 the mines were reopened to work molybdenum and vanadium, which in turn gave way to lead and zinc as ores in the mine, and market prices varied. By 1952, the ores became leaner, lead and zinc prices dropped and inflowing water became a problem. The mines were closed and properties sold to the San Manuel Mine. Mammoth's existence today is dependent on the operation of San Manuel.

The original San Manuel locations were made in 1870, but there was no real development until 1944 after its commercial possibilities had been discovered by the exploration program of the U. S. Geological Survey and the U. S. Bureau of Mines. San Manuel was the first mine to use the active participation of government agencies in long-shot exploration for minerals. It took $100,000,000 and thirteen years' exploration, development, and construction to bring San Manuel into operation. Due to this outlay, however, Magma Copper Company has a thriving concern with a well-laid-out town of over four thousand population.

The copper deposits at Ray were discovered in the 1870's but were not continually and successfully developed until the Ray Consolidated Copper Company was organized in 1906. They developed the mines for working large tonnages of low-grade ore and built a smelter at Hayden. In 1933 the Ray Mines became a division of Kennecott Copper Corporation which continued to develop and expand operations contributing to the growth of Ray and Hayden. Since 1960 the town site of Ray has become a part of the open-pit mining operation, and the residents moved to the town of Kearny near Hayden. Sonora is the residential town for many workers in the Ray mines.

The coming of the railroad created the town of Casa Grande, so named because it was the closest town on the railroad to the Casa Grande ruins. It grew slowly as a cattle shipping point and agricultural center until recent years when it has expanded more rapidly due to the addition of new industries. The selection of Casa Grande as the site of the San Francisco Giants' spring training camp is bringing about a program of construction that will be in excess of six million dollars when completed. This is expected to cause an increase in winter visitors and tourists. Arizona City, a new community for retired people, is being completed and rapid growth is expected.

Coolidge and Eloy are both agricultural centers, coming into existence when the area was developed for farming in the 1920's. As cotton has become more important as a crop and more extensive areas have been irrigated, Coolidge and Eloy have grown to provide cotton gins, shipping and trading centers, and residential centers for farm workers.

Points of Interest: Southwestern Arboretum, Superstition Mountains, Pinal Pioneer Parkway, Picacho Peak, Casa Grande Ruins National Monument, Central Arizona College, Historical County Seat, Arizona State Prison.

County Seat: Florence.

Elevation: 1,500 feet.

SANTA CRUZ COUNTY: Santa Cruz County was a region known well to the many Indian tribes which were its earliest inhabitants. In 1700 it was estimated by the Spanish that there were some five thousand natives populating the region. To these Indians it must have seemed like Paradise with its rolling hills and sheltered canyons, its abundance of wild game, and its flowing streams.

From the early sixteenth century come reports of fair-haired visitors in the Santa Cruz Valley. Spanish Conquistadors, possibly even the famed explorer Cabeza de Vaca, are said to have trekked across the region which is now Southern Arizona.

In 1529 the Franciscan priest Fray Marcos de Niza entered the area near the site of what was to later become Lochiel. Venturing north into what is now Northern Arizona in search of the mythical Seven Cities of Cibola, he returned to Mexico City with glowing accounts of the vast riches to be had. It was these reports that sent the Spanish nobleman and soldier, Francisco Vasquez de Coronado, on his fateful expedition the following year.

For almost another 150 years, no further attempt was made to again enter this land known to the Spanish as "Pimeria Alta"... the upper land of the Pima Indians. In 1687, in an attempt to protect a land passage from Mexico to California through the establishment of missions along the route, Father Eusebio Francisco Kino was sent out to establish the first of what was to become a string of twenty-one missions in Sonora and Southern Arizona. The mission at Tumacacori was established in 1691, after Padres Kino and Salvatierra were asked to the Indian Village by special invitation.

The first permanent white settlement came into being in 1737, with the founding of the Spanish mission rancheria along the banks of the flowing Santa Cruz. Spanish attempts to pronounce the Papage name "Chuevak" came out as Tubac. Fourteen years later, in 1751, the Pima Indians rebelled, killing some one hundred people and destroying Tubac and many other missions in the region. It was this uprising that resulted in the establishment of the First Spanish Garrison in the north, the Presidio San Iganacio de Tubac, built in 1752.

Little activity was seen again until 1758, when Father Garces was sent to the mission at San Xavier del Bac near Tucson. Garces, being an active man, soon began to explore the region. In 1771 he succeeded alone and on foot to cross the Yuma and California deserts and reached the base of the Western Sierras. Upon his return Garces' reports so fired the imagination of Captain Juan Bautista Anza of the Tubac Presidio that he offered to open an overland route to the mission and presidio that had recently been established at Monterey in California.

In 1794 Father Gutierrez arrived at Tumacacori, then head of the district. He found the church "split in two parts," almost in total ruin due to an Apache raid while most of the soldiers at Tubac were on the Anza expedition to California. His life work was to be the building of a new and larger church. Father Gutierrez died in 1820 and although never finished, the noble structure still stands today as a national monument.

After the passing of Father Gutierrez, they were sold, villages and all, for a sum of only $500.00 to a governor of Sonora as "abandoned Pueblo lands." The intense winter of 1848-9 destroyed crops and stock, forcing the few remaining villagers of Tumacacori to finally give up and leave their homes to join kinsmen at neighboring San Xavier.

Falling to ruin Tumacacori stood silent until 1907 when Will C. Barnes, then an assistant U. S. forester, suggested that Tumacacori Mission be made into a National Monument. On September, 1908, President Theodore Roosevelt proclaimed ten acres, including the church and most of the village site, the Tumacacori National Monument.

In 1822, after Mexico obtained its independence from Spain, restrictions upon Americans entering the region of Santa Cruz County were relaxed. The treaty of Guadalupe Hildalgo in 1848, ended a brief war with Mexico and it was the Gadsden Purchase of 1854, which put the entire region under the Flag of the United States.

The memory of tales of the Spanish "Bolas de Platas" beckoned mining men into the region. One of the first to arrive in the new territory was Charles D. Poston in 1856 as a member of the Sonora Exploring and Mining Company. The company took over the empty presidio at Tubac and set up its headquarters. As the little community grew, Poston opened a book of records, performed the marriage ceremonies, baptized the children, and granted divorces.

As soon as it was known that an American company had arrived in Tubac, Mexicans from Sonora came in great numbers to work. Skilled miners could be employed for wages of fifteen to twenty-five dollars per month plus provisions. The Mexican senoritas that also came had a refining influence on the frontier population ... many had been educated at convents and all were practicing Roman Catholics. They called the American men "Los God-Dammes" and the American women "Las Camisas-Coloradas."

However, in June, 1861, with mining machinery running smoothly, with the mines yielding handsomely, and with 250 employees working and being paid, activity in Tubac stopped. With the threat of Civil War, the post of Fort Buchanan, on the Sonoita Creek and at Tubac were ordered abandoned and destroyed. The settlers left and the prosperity of the entire region came to an end.

With the exodus of the United States Army, the Apaches swept across the land driving all but a very few from the region. One hardy soul who remained was Pete Kitchen. He was called a "rough charcoal sketch of a civilized man," and to the wild Apache he was more terrible than an army with banners. His hacienda at the junction of the Santa Cruz River and Potrero Creek was as much a fort as a ranch house.

The frequent Indian raids killed and wounded Kitchen's employees, stole his stock, and studded the skins of his pigs with arrows. In 1871 they killed his son, but the Apache was never able to make the determined Kitchen flee from the valley.

The route from Tucson south into Sonora became known as the way "from Tucson, Tubac, Tumacacori, to Hell."

The end of the Civil War brought back the soldiers and the Apache menace gradually faded away. Apache warfare ended completely in 1886. Although major mines had been discovered before the Civil War, the frequent Indian trouble kept the population and returns low. In 1867 Fort Crittenden was established, overlooking the site of abandoned Fort Buchanan in an attempt to protect the region.

The mining camps of Washington and Duquesne prospered in the 1890's with the extraction of lead, silver, zinc, and copper from the rich earth. One mine, Mt. Mowry near Patagonia, yielded about 1.5 million dollars in silver and lead ore during the period from 1859 to 1862. At one time there were 350 mining claims within a fifteen mile radius of Patagonia.

The cattle industry, originally introduced by the early Jesuit missionaries, expanded throughout the rich grazing ranges with their waist deep grasses. To the Andalusian or Mexican Black-horns of the padres, were added Texas longhorns, then herefords and almost every other known type of beef cattle.

Adding to prosperity of the Santa Cruz Region came the railroad. Rumors that the railroad planned to make Calabasas the port-of-entry into Sonora brought an overnight tent-city. The first brick hotel in the territory was built. The "Tucson Citizen" reported that Calabasas had the "finest hotel west of the Rocky Mountains, and ten or twelve of the best looking Boston-made girls." The Hotel de Santa Rita became known as a popular summer attraction for Tucsonians. So popular that a steamboat line via the Santa Cruz was promoted for a while. When the railroad chose to make Nogales its port-of-entry, the Calabasas tents silently stole away leaving only the prolific wild gourds growing in the area as they were when the first Spanish arrived.

In 1880 Jacob Isaacson, an itinerant peddler from San Francisco, built a small store at the border on the stage route from Tucson to Guaymas. The place which Isaacson picked had in the early days furnished shelter to travelers on the Kino Trail. With its walnut grove in the mountain pass, it was the custom camp at "Los Nogales." Isaacson lived alone, fighting off Apaches and serving the friendly Mexican ranchers and travelers.

In 1881 the Santa Fe Railroad sent out a party of surveyors to extend the line into Mexico. They stopped at the merchant's place which had become known as Isaacson or Issactown. They made it headquarters and the name Isaacson was attached to the post office.

John Brickwood constructed the second permanent building in 1882, a saloon straddling the border making it possible to fix the revenuers by stepping out the back door to do business. This practice ceased in 1907 when a sixty foot by two mile "Public Reservation" was created by Presidential Proclamation.

The future of the border city, by then called "Line City", was assured in 1882 when the New Mexico and Arizona Railroad joined the Sonora Line. The day the railroad lines joined, two engines met at the border facing each other and the last spike, a silver one, was driven. The railroad called their new station "Nogales," which seemed to settle the name. The citizens petitioned to have the post office name changed from Isaacson to Nogales. In 1893 the town became incorporated.

In 1895 the growth of Nogales and the development of mines in the vicinity resulted in the necessity for greater communication between the area and its county government. However, at that time, being part of Pima County, one was forced to travel to and from the county seat in Tucson by way of the railroad through Sonoita and Fairbank, a trip taking almost a day. Thus came the demand for local government and the creation of a new county to be called Grant County. Finally on January 25, 1899, after some year's delay, a bill for the creation of a county was introduced to the Territorial Assembly. On March 15, 1899, Santa Cruz County was established with Nogales chosen as the County Seat. Nogales has an elevation of 3,800 feet.

YAVAPAI COUNTY: Yavapai County was one of the four counties created by the First Arizona Territorial Legislature on November 8, 1864. It originally included about half of the entire Territory, but was divided repeatedly, so that now, all or part of nine of Arizona's present fourteen counties were, at one time, part of Yavapai. All but one of these nine counties are now larger than Yavapai, which has an area of 5,179,240 acres. The name Yavapai is from an Indian Tribe and means "sun people." The county seat is Prescott. which was also the Territorial Capital from 1864 to 1867 and from 1887 to 1889. Almost half of Yavapai County is in national forests.

Yavapai County has long been famous for fabulous placers and mines as well as its lumber resources and stock raising areas. Tourism, in Prescott, Mingus Mountain, and the Verde Valley has become increasingly important in recent years with the completion of Black Canyon Highway. A large cement plant, providing cement for construction at Glen Canyon Dam, has aided the economy of the county. Other new firms recently started or planned include a pole-treating plant and a motion picture equipment and supplies manufacturing firm.

The only established community that has continued to grow through the years is Prescott. When the governor of the new Arizona Territory arrived at Fort Whipple in December, 1863, he decided that the seat of the new government should be near the fort. Accordingly, the Territorial Capital was established on May 30, 1864, a few miles from Fort Whipple. It was named Prescott in honor of William H. Prescott the American historian and authority on Aztec and Spanish-American history. Two things about the early community of Prescott made it unique in Arizona: it was built entirely of wood, and almost all of its inhabitants were Americans. It is believed to be the birthplace of rodeos, which grew out of the annual Fourth of July celebrations held every year since 1864.

Walker is the next town to be listed in the census (1880). It was the center of extensive mining operations between 1875 and 1890 in the Bradshaw Mountains. The rich Congress Mine was discovered in 1883, creating the town of Congress, and later the railroad established Congress Junction as an ore shipping point. With the working out of the richest ores and the drop in the price of silver, mining decreased and both Walker and Congress became ghost towns. Congress Junction still exists today as a very small shipping point for cattle.

Claims in the Jerome area were filed and mining was started as early as 1873, but true development of that area had to wait for the railroad. In 1883 the United Verde Copper Company built a road to connect with the railroad at Ash Fork in order to bring in smelter equipment. The town established by the mine and smelter was named Jerome in honor of Eugene Jerome of New York, treasurer of the company. In 1886 William A. Clark bought the properties and built a narrow gauge railroad connection to Ash Fork. He developed and operated the United Verde Company very successfully in spite of fire that could not be put out in some of the tunnels.

In 1912 James S. Douglas, son of Dr. James Douglas of Phelps Dodge, and Major Pickrell became major stockholders in the United Verde Extension, the former "Little Daisy" claim. They and George Tener of Pittsburgh developed it, and it broke into a true bonanza of forty-five percent copper. Like all bonanzas, this was an extremely rich development as long as it lasted but was exhausted by the late 1920's. In 1919 the United Verde Extension built a smelter and smelter town named Clemenceau, but it died when the United Verde Extension ran out of ore. It was never listed in the U. S. Census.

Tremendous blasting in the Black Pit Mine in 1925 caused Jerome to start sliding downhill, literally and figuratively. The concrete jail skidded slowly three hundred feet across the highway and tumbled on its side below street level. Citizens of Jerome shored up the buildings, but the slump in copper prices in the 1930's spelled the end of Jerome as an important mining community. Today, Jerome is being preserved as a ghost town and museum center for tourists.

Clarkdale (named after William Clark, owner of the United Verde Mine) was established as the smelter town for the United Verde, Jerome Verde, and Verde Central Companies. With the closing of the mines, Clarkdale was expected to die. However, since the town was owned by the mining company, it was sold. The new owner kept it alive by converting it into a community for retired people until new industry gave it a new life. The Phoenix Cement plant was established in Clarkdale in 1958 and insured the continued existence of the community.

Principal Industries: livestock, mining, tourism.

Points of Interest: Smoki Museum, Granite Dells, Jerome, Tuzigoot National Monument, Montezuma Castle National Monument, Montezuma Well, Camp Verde, Horse Thief Basin, Joshua Forest Parkway, Yavapai College, Prescott College.
County Seat: Prescott.
Elevation: 5,410 feet.

YUMA COUNTY: Yuma is the most western county in Arizona. It is bordered on the west by California and on the south by Mexico. Yuma County is predominantly desert interspersed with rugged mountains. However, there is an abundance of arable land in the valley regions.

The warm, dry climate provides an extended agricultural season and year-round recreation. Temperatures range from the upper nineties to the lower hundreds from May through September, and from the low forties to the middle eighties the rest of the year. The average annual temperature is fifty-two degrees in the north and sixty degrees in the south.

77

The city of Yuma is located in the southwest corner of the county. Due to the twisting of the Colorado River and the unusual placement of the United States-Mexican border, California lies to the north of Yuma and Mexico lies to the west. Most of the city is situated atop a mesa which extends south from the Arizona-California border. The fertile valleys which surround the mesa form the nucleus of the county's agricultural land.

The earliest economic development of the area which now comprises Yuma County was based on mining and trade. Colorado River crossings near the sites of present-day Yuma city attracted travelers and miners. As the West became more populated and mining along the Colorado less productive, agriculture superceded mining as a major source of income. During World War II and after, government employment rose to prominence with the establishment of military testing and training facilities.

Today, agriculture, military installations, tourism, and light manufacturing form the economic base for Yuma County. Agriculture is by far the leading sector. Alfalfa, cotton, sorghums, and citrus are the most important crops. Average annual agricultural employment was 9,225 in 1969, and farm income has been in excess of seventy-five million dollars for the past five years. Two military installations contribute significantly to Yuma's well-being. Yuma Proving Ground, the world's largest military installation, is located thirty miles northeast of Yuma. The Marine Corps Air Station, outside Yuma, adds an additional dimension annually to the economy besides providing many civilian jobs. Tourism is another major source of income in the county. Although no recent estimates of income from tourism are available, large numbers of visitors come in the fall and winter months taking advantage of the mild climate and recreation. Service industries account for nearly ten percent of total employment. Manufacturing, although limited, does play an important role in the economy, producing photo equipment, textiles, and paper products.

Economic indicators point to a steady rate of economic growth. Per capita effective buying income, bank deposits, and retail sales have shown continuous growth. Most sectors of the economy anticipate a moderate growth in employment or will remain stable.

The best prospects for future economic growth in Yuma County lie in the areas of trade, services, and manufacturing.

Principal Industries: agriculture, mining, cattle feeding, tourism, government business.

Points of Interest: Arizona Western College, Yuma Territorial Prison.

County Seat: Yuma.

Elevation: 138 feet.

LA PAZ COUNTY: Founded in 1983 it is the youngest of the fifteen counties. The county has an area of about 4,430 square miles. It takes its name from the first county seat for Yuma county. At one time the city of La Paz was a famous mining town. About 80% of the land in present day La Paz County is owned by the federal government.

Points of Interest: Colorado Indian Reservation, Alamo State Park, Buckskin State Park, Parker Dam, Kofa Game Range.

County Seat: Parker

We have all heard of Ghost Towns. In the 15 counties of Arizona there are many ghost towns. The author wishes to call your attention to some south of Tucson which have a rich history and fun to visit and explore. You can visit Cerro Colorado, site of the gold mining of the 1850's; Arivaca a semi-ghost town with some interesting buildings. Oro Blanco is a noted stage stop dating from the 1870's. Ruby is one of the better known ghost towns in all of southern Arizona. Helvetia, Greaterville, and Alto are also in the Tucson area and while they were not large towns, they played a significant part in Arizona's early history. If you want to really admire the pioneer spirit, then you must head farther west near Salome, Arizona. There you can find ghost towns like Harqua Hala, Swansea and Signal. These were lonely and barren little towns and about as western as they can be. You will have to admire the courage and the real American spirit of those pioneers who pushed West to live and die in those God-forsaken places.

CHAPTER 10.

Military Outposts of the West

"It is said that a wicked soldier died in Yuma and was consigned to the fiery regions for his manifold sins; but unable to stand the rigors of the climate, sent back for his blankets."

J. Ross Brown
Adventures in the
Apache Country, 1864

Arizona was a hardship post for the military. Anyone who was sent to this land of sand and gila monsters, was almost considered punished by his superiors. No one really wanted to serve here at one of the many posts. While some had the spirit of adventure, very few really wanted to chase and kill or be killed by the Indians. After all, what did one do at an army post in the summer time? The nights are long when the temperatures zooms over a hundred degrees. It is difficult to sleep. Day time temperatures were worse. It is true that some of the forts were located in northern Arizona where the temperatures were cooler. But the loneliness of a frontier was a difficult adjustment. Women were few and there really was little social life with the opposite sex. It was like being sent to Siberia. Women simply refused to come to live in Indian territory.

Hiram C. Hodge, writing in his book, *1877 Arizona as it Was,* has this to say:

"Recognizing the fact that no community or country can ever enter upon its highest state of prosperity, refinement, or happiness without the aid and assistance of woman, Arizona and her citizens would welcome the advent of large numbers of the true, the pure, the good, of the superabundant females of other portions of the Union, and would give them a welcome such as goddesses might envy."

Despite the cruel hardships of the area, the American soldier wrote many a glorious chapter in the unfolding of the West. His bravery and his cunning was well known to the historians of the West.

The Army posts played a big role in the history of Arizona. Many of them are famous. Without them Arizona would never have survived. Their prime role was to defend the Americans from the attacks of the Indians. And this they did with fervor. In the early days of Arizona, they were probably better known as Forts. To wit, we shall mention the better known ones.

Fort Apache is in the White Mountain country. It has an altitude of six thousand feet. Its original name was Camp Ord. Founded in 1870, it was active until about 1924.

Fort Bowie was established in 1863 and for many years it was one of the most important posts in the Territory, being surrounded by hostile Indians. It was the headquarters for General Crook and his negotiations with Cochise. In 1886 Geronimo surrendered near the Fort. The fort was abandoned in 1894.

Fort Mohave is on the Colorado River, 325 miles above Yuma. It was established in 1858 and abandoned when the Civil War began. It was reopened a few years later to protect the local citizenry and closed permanently in 1890.

Fort McDowell, located about fifty miles east of Phoenix, was opened in 1865. It was renamed after General Irvin McDowell. It was from here that one of the early founders of Phoenix, John Y. T. Smith, carried on a hay business. The fort closed around the year 1890.

Fort Yuma is located in Yuma, and of all the forts, it must be considered the most strategic. In 1850, Major S. P. Hintzelman came to the Yuma site and was stationed at Camp Independence on the eastern bank of the Colorado River. The arrival of these soldiers was the beginning of Fort Yuma. The army leader called his camp Fort Independence, but by March, 1851, the troops had moved to the area of the old Spanish mission, and this place was soon named Fort Yuma.

Had it not been for the army establishing Fort Yuma at the confluence of the Gila and Colorado Rivers, doubtless the history of this country, in fact, the history of the entire west, might have been vastly different. The Indians would never have been allowed the white settlement to remain. Neither would they have allowed the thousands of immigrants to cross the desert of their domain unmolested. During the early history of the tiny white settlements, the Indians did rise up on occasion and kill or drive the inhabitants out, including the soldiers. It was only after the army garrisoned the fort with a large force that the Yuma Indians ceased resistance.

In 1986, the old army depot in Yuma, nearly 120 years old, was added to the state's parks system. It once doubled as a family home and office for the National Weather Services. The site now known as the Army Quartermaster Depot, over the years was also known as a military-supply storage site and was a post for the International Boundary Commission. The park will provide live representations of what life was like near the confluence of the Gila and Colorado Rivers during 10 periods between 1500 and 1912.

The Army built the Quartermaster Depot in 1864 to serve as a supply warehouse for goods destined for Arizona, New Mexico, Nevada, Utah and Texas. Goods arrived on paddle steamers and were unloaded and stored in the adobe structure. It was a very busy place and hired as many as seventy civilians.

Presently Fort McDowell is being reconstructed according to the 1879 plan at Pioneer Arizona, a living history museum. Reconstruction is currently in progress. The museum is located about seventeen miles north of Phoenix on Interstate 17. This historical museum has twenty seven buildings including a blacksmith shop and original homes from the era of 1860 to 1890. It is open daily except for Christmas Day. This is an educational center where Arizona's pioneer heritage lives daily.

CHAPTER 11.

Famous Arizona Governors

Evan Mecham (1986-1988)

After 12 years of Democratic rule under Democratic governors, Evan Mecham, a Republican, and a Mormon, was elected governor of Arizona in 1986. He is the first automobile dealer to ever hold this high office. He was born on May 12, 1924, in Duchesne, Utah. He is married and is the father of seven children. He attended Arizona State University and was a fighter pilot in WWII. He was a prisoner of war in WWII in Germany for 22 days. He was elected to the state senate in 1960. In 1962 he lost an election to the U.S. Senate to Carl Hayden who was to serve in congress longer than any other citizen in our history. In 1964 he ran for governor and lost to Democrat Sam Goddard. He ran again in 1974, 1978, 1982 and in 1986, he won with only 40% of the vote. One of his first acts was to rescind the Martin Luther King holiday in Arizona. Among many reasons given, the Governor did not think that he deserved a paid holiday in Arizona. This opened a long debate in political circles. Within a short time in office, he was facing recall, impeachment from office and a criminal trial. As time went on he managed to offend the Blacks, the Jews, women, Hispanics, orientals and the news media. Many of his political appointees had dubious qualifications and he attacked the "establishment". He was finally impeached and Rose Mofford became governor on April 5, 1988. She was the first woman governor in Arizona history. Of all the politicians that held high office in Arizona, Evan Mecham holds a special place.

Many of his followers believe that he was impeached by a corrupt legislature who later fell prey to the AZscam scandals and legal convictions in the courts to some of its members. He begged for money nationwide, saying he had fallen victim to liberals, homosexuals and Democrats. He asked conservatives outside of Arizona to pack their bags and move to Arizona to help him. In 1992 he was on the ballot and ran for the U.S. Senate as an independent against the incumbent, Senator John McCain.

Rawghlie Clement Stanford (1937-1938)

He was born in 1878 in Buffalo Gap, Texas. He arrived in Arizona in 1881 and worked as a miner and as a cowboy. He served as a volunteer in the Spanish American War. As a self-educated lawyer, he gained the esteem of his fellow citizens and was elected Maricopa County Judge. As governor he was involved in three special sessions in 1937, as he battled for a revision of the sales tax. The mining companies were fighting to starve off the hike. Other controversies involved the highway patrol and an alleged Governor's Relief Fund. Stanford later served as a member of the Arizona Supreme Court. He died in 1968.

Thomas E. Campbell (1919-22)

He was a native of Prescott and the first native-born Arizonan to serve in the legislature. He had served as assessor of Yavapai County and as a State Tax Commissioner before becoming governor. He is the only governor in the history of Arizona who served one year without pay (1916), because the election was contested. He made another bid for the governor's chair in 1936 but failed. His nickname was Traveling Tom. He died in 1944.

Jack R. Williams (1967-1974)

A popular radio announcer and executive in Phoenix, Jack Williams became the fifth Republican governor by defeating Sam Goddard in the 1966 campaign. In 1970 he became the first four-year governor in the history of the State after the legislature lengthened the terms of some of the high state officials. He was embroiled in controversy after signing a disputed Farm Labor Bill. Known for his conservatism, he took great pride in fiscal responsibility and maintained budget surpluses each year. He served as mayor of Phoenix from 1956 to 1960. He lives in retirement in Phoenix.

Bruce Babbitt (1978-1986)

Assumed office after death of Governor Bolin. He is the son of a prosperous family in Flagstaff. He received a geology degree from Notre Dame University, a masters degree in geophysics from the University of Newcastle in England, and a law degree from Harvard University. He was a strong contender for the Democratic nomination for the Presidency in 1988. As Governor he left a strong legacy of vigorous leadership and set an active tone of success.

CHAPTER 12.

Arizona Congressmen and the Executive Branch

"The land taken over in the Gadsden Treaty in Arizona was so desolate, deserted and God-forsaken that a wolf could not make a living upon it."
Kit Carson

The Arizona delegation to the United States Congress is an extraordinary one with very capable and distinguished lawmakers. Two of the present members have national reputations and Arizona can be proud of its outstanding representation in Congress.

Senator Dennis DeConcini — He was born in Tucson in 1937. He attended public schools in Tucson and Phoenix and received his Bachelors and law degrees from the University of Arizona. After a tour of duty in the U. S. Army as a Lieutenant in 1959, he entered private practice of law with his father, a former justice of the Arizona Supreme Court. He was special counsel to the governor in 1965, and served as Pima County Attorney. He is married to the former Susan Hurley and they have three children. The senior Senator was elected to the Senate in 1976. He is a Democrat.

John McCain — Republican Senator who took office in the U. S. Senate on January 1, 1987. He replaced Senator Barry Goldwater. He was born on August 29, 1936, in the Panama Canal Zone. Senator McCain is a graduate of the Naval Academy and a former navy pilot. In Vietnam he was a prisoner of war for 5½ years. His father and grandfather were admirals in the Navy. The Senator retired from the Navy in 1981 as a Captain. After being in Arizona a very short time, he won a seat in Congress in 1982 and again in 1984. His campaign for the U. S. Senate took in more than two million dollars. His political ideology follows President Reagan and President Bush although occasionally he votes the other way.

Fife Symington — Fife Symington, the 19th Governor of Arizona, was inaugurated on March 6, 1991, after winning an unprecedented special runoff general election. His two year gubernatorial campaign was founded on a commitment to bring Arizona fiscal responsibility, education reform, and environmental protection.

Symington was born in New York City on August 12, 1945, Raised in Maryland, he comes from a prominent political family. Symington attended Gilman Country Day and earned a Bachelor's Degree in Liberal Arts from Harvard University in 1968. As a Harvard student, he was an active supporter of Barry Goldwater's 1964 Presidential Campaign.

Symington was first introduced to Arizona in 1968, whin he was assigned to Luke Air Force Base as a United States Air Force Second Lieutenant.

Bob Stump — Congressman was born in Phoenix on April 4, 1927. He attended elementary school in Phoenix and high school in Tolleson. He attended Arizona State University and received a degree in Agronomy in 1951. During World War II he served in the U. S. Navy. Mr. Stump has for many years been a cotton and grain farmer in the Tolleson, Arizona, area. In 1958 he was elected to the Arizona House of Representatives where he served for eight years. He was president of the Senate in 1975 and 1976. Mr. Stump has three children: Karen, Bob, and Bruce. He was elected to his first term in the U. S. House of Representatives on November of 1976. He is a Republican. Congressman Stump represents District Three.

Karen English — The newly created 6th district in the U.S. Congress is represented by Karen English. She is a moderated Democrat who was born in Berkeley, California in 1973, is married and has two children and three stepchildren. She was a Coconino County Board of Supervisors from 1981 to 1987; Arizona House 1987-1991; Senate 1991-1993. She was elected to Congress in 1992 and is serving her first term. She is a strong advocate of environmental issues, abortion rights and in her initial campaign for Congress, she enjoyed the endorsement of former Senator Barry Goldwater, the retired Senator from Arizona. She is a very genial, popular and very competent legislator.

John Kyl — Republican Congressman who represents District Four. Born on April 25, 1942, in Oakland, Nebraska, he received his Bachelors and law degrees from the University of Arizona. He is married and has two children. Congressman Kyl is a fiscal conservative and follows President Reagan's ideology. He was a partner in the law firm of Jennings, Strouss and Salmon.

Jim Kolbe — Republican Congressman from District Five. First elected to Congress in 1984. He was born on June 29, 1942, in Evanston, Illinois. Received his Bachelors degree in political science from Northwestern University and his Masters degree in business administration from Stanford University. He served in the U. S. Navy in Vietnam and was discharged in 1969. He served in the Arizona Senate for three terms.

Ed Pastor — A native Arizonian, Ed Pastor was born in Claypool, Arizona, on June 28, 1943. He earned his juris doctorate in 1974 and bachelor of arts degree in chemistry in 1966 from Arizona State University.

He was elected to the Maricopa Board of Supervisors in 1976 and took office in January 1977. He was re-elected in 1980, 1984, and 1988. He resigned on May 6, 1991, to run for Congress from Arizona's 2nd district.

He was elected to serve the people of the 2nd Congressional District on September 24, 1991. He serves on the Committee on Small Business, Education and Labor and the Select Committee on Aging.

Sam Coppersmith — A Democratic congressman representing District One. Born on May 22, 1955, he graduated from Harvard University in 1976 and holds a law degree from Yale University. He is a first term congressman in a heavy Republican district. He is the first Democrat elected in that district since 1950. He favors abortion rights and holds very strict conservative views on money matters as do most of the voters whom he represents. This is the first time he has held political office. He has chosen to run for the U.S. Senate as a Democrat in the 1994 election.

CHAPTER 13.

Arizona Cities

You can search the whole world to find a state like Arizona. You will find none.

Frank Chiappetta

Just about every city in Arizona has a history that would take a volume to fill. They all played a part in molding this great state.

The following is a short story of some of the cities.

THE PHOENIX STORY

Many say that Phoenix is the most desirable place to live in the United States. Phoenix is certainly a very beautiful city and its proximity to Mexico, Los Angeles, Las Vegas, and even Disneyland makes it a Mecca for tourists. And its celebrated climate of having about 340 sunny days in the year is world famous. Projections show that Phoenix will have a population of 2 million people in 1990. The metropolitan area covers 270 square miles and it has adequate motels and hotels to accommodate the host of tourists who come each year. It is home to the famous Arizona State University (about 41,000 students) although the University is actually in Tempe, Arizona, a suburban area next to Phoenix.

From its beginnings a century ago, Phoenix has repeatedly outgrown the dreams and hopes of its citizens. Today she stands as a majestic metropolis, too preoccupied with jet age expansion to remember the days when she was but a spot in the vast desert. Phoenix was and is one of the fastest growing cities in the country.

THE SAGUARO (pronounced sah-war-oh) grows only in Arizona and Mexico with a few scattered along the Colorado River in California. Its blossom is Arizona's state flower. This cactus grows to a height of 40 to 50 feet and lives to an age of 150 to 200 years.

Justice Sandra Day O'Conner of the U.S. Supreme Court

Dennis DeConcini is a member of a family with a long history in government, law and business. In 1972 he was elected Pima County attorney and quickly established himself as a crimefighter, especially against organized crime figures. In 1976 he was elected to the U.S. Senate following the retirement of Paul Fannin.

Bruce Babbitt, governor of Arizona 1978-1987. Babbitt, scion of the merchantile-ranching family, earned high marks during his nine year tenure and must be considered one of the best governors in the state history. He presently is Secretary of the Interior in the Cabinet of President Bill Clinton. (Photo courtesy, Bruce Babbitt)

Navajo Nation Fair, inter-tribal pow-wow. (Photo, Kenji Kawano)

Evan Mecham, former governor of Arizona. His stunning upset of House Majority leader Burton Barr ("the most powerful man in Arizona") in the Republican Primary in 1986 is considered one of the most surprising in the history of the state. Mecham came to Arizona during World War II for pilot training. After the war he moved to Glendale and opened a car dealership.

Palo Verde Nuclear Generating Station, Wintersburg, Arizona

Charles Barkley of the Phoenix Suns, the most popular man in Arizona.

Scenic view in northern Arizona. (Arizona Office of Tourism)

l to r: Barry Goldwater, Carl Hayden and Paul Fannin discussing issues that affect Arizona. The state maintains a proud record of being well-represented in Washington. Since statehood on 1912 several senators and congressmen have held leadership roles and not one has been tainted by even a minor scandal. (Arizona Historical Foundation)

Arizona Medal of Honor winners, l to r: George Day (Vietnam), Sylvestre Herrera (WWII), Fred Ferguson (Vietnam), Jay Vargas (Vietnam).

At an Americanism dinner in 1953, Barry Goldwater, Governor Howard Pyle and John Rhodes discussing issues of the day with Senator Joseph McCarthy of Wisconsin (2nd from right). (Arizona Historical Foundation)

Carved Hopi Indian kachina dolls, symbolic of the tribe's ancient ceremonies, are among the many items reflecting Arizona's Indian cultures. (Arizona Office of Tourism)

THE STATELY RUIN OF SAN CAYETANO DEL TUMACACORI lies just south of Tubac and is open daily to the public. The mission model silhouetted in the foreground depicts the magnificent mission grounds in the days of the Franciscans in the early 1800's. (Arizona Office of Tourism)

SERGEANT JOHN CAMPBELL is pictured at the 100th anniversary celebration at Fort Huachuca in March, 1977.

Senator John McCain

Former Senator Barry Goldwater with author's wife, Carol Woznicki.

Governor Franklin Roosevelt, Eleanor Roosevelt, Isabella Greenway and Senator Thomas Walsh of Arizona, September 28, 1932 at the Greenway ranch in Williams, Arizona. (Arizona Historical Society/Tucson)

Sidney P. Osborn is considered by many historians to be one of Arizona's best governors. He is the only one elected to four consecutive terms. He was at the helm during the turbulent World War II years that brought unprecedented change to the state. (Arizona State Library)

Senator McCain greets President Nixon.

The author in his apartment at the University of Beijing, China.

Tubac, Arizona, famous fort established there in 1752. (Arizona Office of Tourism)

Tawa Centre in Scottsdale.

"Break, Western Style." (Arizona Office of Tourism)

Frank Gordon, presiding judge, Chief Justice Arizona Supreme Court, trial of Evan Mecham. (Photo courtesy of Arizona Republic)

Howard Pyle was a popular radio personality before being elected governor in 1950. For years he broadcast on NBC, the famous Easter Sunrise Service from the Grand Canyon. During WWII Pyle was a war correspondent and was on the battleship Missouri when the Japanese formally surrendered. Pyle, a Republican, was only the third governor from that party since statehood and his election marks the beginning of the two-party system in state politics. His campaign manager in 1950 was a young political novice named Barry Goldwater. (Arizona Historical Foundation)

The first settlers in the Phoenix area were the Hohokam Indians who built networks of irrigation ditches and used water of the Salt River. Some of these ditches are still in use today. What became of the Hohokam Indians remains a mystery.

The first white settler to arrive in Phoenix was a certain John Y. T. Smith. Because of the canals left by the Hohokam tribe, Smith decided to settle here.

In the spring of 1867, Jack Swilling, a friend from Wickenburg, visited Smith and was impressed by the irrigation ditches. Swilling returned in the fall with men to enlarge one of the canals and by the next year, the Salt River Valley Canal extended several miles west of the Salt River. Now, with almost thirty people settled in the area, it needed a name.

Darrell Duppa, an educated Englishman, suggested the mythical name which was unanimously accepted by the founding fathers in 1870. The Phoenix bird was a symbol of immortality to the ancient Egyptians. It was their belief that every five hundred years this bird set himself afire, then rose again from his own ashes. It was the disappearance of the Hohokam Tribe five hundred years earlier which prompted Duppa's suggestion. He is reported to have said, "Let us call it Phoenix, for here on the ruins of the old, a new city will arise."

Phoenix was officially filed as a townsite in 1872. The same year the first dry goods store was opened, owned and operated by the Goldwater family. Cotton cultivation began the next year — thus starting the agricultural industry. This industry became the main source of income in Phoenix for many years.

In 1887 the arrival of the first railroad advanced the phenomenal growth of agriculture. Two years later, Phoenix became the Territorial Capitol. In 1900 Phoenix was truly a capitol with a growing population of 5,554. Ten years later this figure had more than doubled.

In 1911 with the completion of the Theodore Roosevelt Dam, the growth of this desert oasis began in earnest. Roosevelt Lake assured the city of an ample water supply. One year later — Phoenix became the State Capitol of Arizona — as Arizona became the forty-eighth State.

World War I gave Arizona's cotton, produce, and cattle farmers a big shot in the arm. This prosperity caused Phoenix's population to almost triple to a figure of 29,053 by 1920.

Phoenix, now a modern city, had its first regularly scheduled flight service in 1927. However, the spirit of the Old West was back three years later, with the advent of the first rodeo in Phoenix. These two items, coupled with an average annual temperature of seventy degrees and only seven and one-half inches of rain, helped bring a new source of revenue ... the seasonal tourist trade.

World War II temporarily slowed down the tourist business, but it did bring Phoenix's second big growth. By 1945, greater Phoenix had a population of over 160,000. All these people created a need for a new source of revenue. So Phoenix, now a true metropolis, started to industrialize.

Today Phoenix stands as a majestic, desert giant. With a population of about 1 million, it is the twentieth largest city in the United States. A new civilization has indeed sprung from the ashes of the past.

The best way to describe Phoenix is in the following way: Phoenix is modern, youthful, and growing. These three words provide an accurate description of the population. The vast majority of area residents are active adults between the ages of eighteen and fifty. In fact, six of every ten adults are less than fifty and four out of ten adults are between eighteen and thirty-five. The majority of newcomers to this city are under thirty-five.

Tourism and travel play a major role in the economy of Metro Phoenix. They generate over a billion dollars a year in revenue. Manufacturing is first and most people are not aware of this. After all in many minds, how could manufacturing plants thrive in the desert along with cactus and sand? Tourists who come to Arizona are most often from the Eastern states, and California. But many people living in the Midwest, find Phoenix an irresistible attraction. Certainly the horrible winter of 1977 turned many eyes from the east to the west. From all indications the tourist industry in the state of Arizona is just beginning.

Three outstanding concert halls, Phoenix Civic Plaza's Symphony Hall, Scottsdale's Center for the Performing Arts, and Grady Gammage Auditorium located on the campus of Arizona State University provide the Phoenix area with excellent facilities for concerts by internationally renowned artists, live performances by theatre groups, and other diverse community sponsored events.

Frank Lloyd Wright's Taliesin West and Paolo Soleri's Cosanti Foundation are the enchanting architectural dreams of two of the world's great artisans.

Metro Phoenix is the home of the NBA Phoenix Suns, PCL Phoenix Firebirds, Phoenix Open golf tournament, and major league baseball in the famed Cactus League. The Fiesta Bowl and parade has attracted national and international attention. In 1987, some 70 million TV viewers watched the national championship broadcast from Tempe. Dog racing, horse racing, auto racing, regattas and professional rodeos, some of the finest in the world, are also well attended. Individuals can play tennis, golf, bowl, hunt, swim during most of the year, motor boat, water ski, shoot skeet, fish, and ski and play in the snow by driving north about two hours.

Eighty four percent own their own homes. About ten percent of the people live in mobile homes and the remaining six percent reside in townhouses and other multiple type units.

Five years ago, sixty percent of the households in Metro Phoenix did not live in their present housing unit. The high mobility of the residents characterizes Phoenix as an active, constantly changing market.

In 1986 Phoenix ranked sixteenth for comparative living costs for an urban family of four among major urban centers in America.

GLENDALE

Established in 1892 and incorporated in 1910, Glendale is located west of Phoenix. It enjoys an enviable, healthful business climate. It is the center of Arizona's huge fresh produce industry, being the largest shipping point in the state for fruit and vegetables. Broadly diversified industry contributes over sixty percent to the real income of the area. Luke Air Force Base, a permanent base, is also a major economic factor. Glendale shares the tremendous growth of Arizona with a population approaching 150,000 people.

Five miles north of downtown Glendale is the famed, American Graduate School of International Management. The school was founded in 1946, originally under the name of the American Institute for Foreign Trade. This is the only graduate school in the United States devoted exclusively to training men and women for international management careers. The school has over 9,000 alumni, of which two-thirds are or have been working and living in approximately one hundred countries around the world.

91

Glendale Community College is located on 160 acres two miles north of downtown Glendale, where it serves the citizens of western Maricopa County.

One of the more famous high schools in the State of Arizona is Glendale High School.

Classes were held in 1911 in a storeroom which was situated on the present site of the Glendale City Hall parking area. In 1912 bonds were authorized to build the permanent school on the present grounds. Over the years, the contributions of the high school have been enormous to the Valley of the Sun and to the State of Arizona.

Starting with Glendale High School, the area now has a total of nine high schools and it is known as the Glendale Unified School District. Dr. Jerry George is the able and very genial Superintendent of Schools. The district has about 12,800 students. Of all the school districts in the State of Arizona, it is considered by teachers, students, and parents to be number one.

SCOTTSDALE

The glamour of Scottsdale as a tourist city and a fine place to live is known all over the world. Of all the cities in Arizona, most people will identify Scottsdale as being one city they have heard of someplace in their travels or readings. And what a wonderful city it is! It was incorporated in 1951 with a land area less than one square mile and with only two thousand people. Today its population approaches close to 150,000 covering an area over eighty-nine square miles. Although tourism is a key factor in the economy of the "West's most western town," Scottsdale's economic makeup has become well diversified. Electronic manufacturing plants and new industrial locations have broadened the economic base. Scottsdale is a leader in neighborhood development and has just completed a new, civic mall and fine arts center designed to serve the needs of all sections of the community. Although growing at an impressive rate, Scottsdale has not lost the friendliness of a small western community. The climate and its abundance of recreational and cultural activities satisfy a diversity of interests. These are factors creating the dynamic, yet informal, life style that is uniquely Scottsdale. Anyone visiting Arizona, somehow ends up visiting this celebrated city.

Scottsdale's "Parada del Sol" Rodeo and its famous horse shows help maintain its western image.

Scottsdale is attracting industry with very strict pollution standards. Its airport is expanding and it will rival Tucson and Phoenix someday.

Scottsdale likes horses. Bridle paths, stables, exercise tracks, and equestrian arenas are everywhere. Scottsdale's schools are some of the finest in the nation. And the city is very proud of Scottsdale Community College.

The city has also become a great place for retirees. The senior citizens flock to this city of hospitality and love.

SHOW LOW

Arizona has many unique cities. One of the more dynamic, small towns is Show Low. It is located 195 miles north east of Phoenix.

The story of how the city received its name is an interesting one. The town got its name when C. E. Cooley and Marion Clark decided to dissolve their partnership. By playing a game of cards they were to decide who was to move. Clark is supposed to have said, "If you show low, you win." Cooley turned up the deuce of clubs and replied, "Show low it is."

With an elevation of 6,500 feet, this White Mountain Community was established in 1880 and incorporated in 1953.

Tourism and recreation are important to the economy of Show Low. Due to its size and location, the community serves as a regional trade and services center for Southern Navajo County and portions of Southern Apache County. It also is an entry point to the White Mountain recreation areas for most visitors.

Most Show Low manufacturing employment is in the forest products industry. The Reidhead Lumber Mill employs many people.

Northland Pioneer College began serving Navajo County during the 1974-75 school year. The state accredited community college has adopted the mini-center concept and will initially have centers in Holbrook, Winslow, Snowflake, and Show Low.

Show Low is surrounded by many year-round, recreational opportunities and points of scenic interest. The Apache Sitgreaves National Forest, Fort Apache Indian Reservation, and the scenic White Mountain and Mogollon Rim areas are nearby for campers and fishermen. Boating and fishing are popular in many lakes and streams, including Tools Hollow Lake, Rainbow Lake, Show Low Lake, and White Mountain Lake.

TUBAC

Tubac, Arizona, could be called the St. Augustine, Florida, of the Far West. It was the first European settlement in Arizona when the Viceroy in Mexico City ordered a military establishment to protect the missions and mines in that area.

In 1773 the Presidio's Commander, Captain Juan Bautista de Anza, established an overland route between Tubac and what is now Los Angeles. Two years later a colonizing party with women and children left Tubac and marched to California's Golden Gate where the way was paved for the founding of San Francisco.

The first school west of the Atlantic coast line is said to have been established in Tubac.

A party of Mormons founded a small community in Tubac in 1789.

In its early years the very elite in Arizona lived in Tubac. Many of its early settlers came from Germany. In 1859 a post office was established and Arizona's first newspaper, the Weekly Arizonian, was published. For many years it was called the San Francisco of the West.

Charles D. Poston, who would be known as the "Father of Arizona," set up headquarters of the Sonora Exploring and Mining Company in this city in 1856.

Today Tubac is a big art colony. So many artists came to Tubac that they formed the Santa Cruz Valley Art Association.

There are some interesting excursions to the Tumacacori National Monument, to historic Tubac State Park, and to the Washington Camp ghost town.

AMADO

Not far from the city of Tubac is the small city of Amado. While not as famous as Tubac it was founded in 1910 by Manuel H. Amado. He established a store and a post office on the Tucson-Nogales branch of the railway. An interesting little church was built there in 1951 by Father Fredrick Curry, a retired Priest of the Tucson Catholic Diocese. The author was there when the first Mass in that church was celebrated. It reflects today the zeal and pioneer spirit of Father Curry.

TUCSON

Tucson's roots are bedded deep in the past, so deep in fact that some historians believe it to be the oldest continually inhabited city in the United States. Archeologists have found evidence of Indian civilizations dating back to at least 900 A.D.

The recorded history of this picturesque desert city is colorful and dates back to 1539, when Mendoza, the Spanish Viceroy of Mexico, dispatched Fray Marcos de Niza in search of the Seven Cities of Cibola. The latter's glowing report of his journey led Don Francisco Vasquez Coronado's famous expedition and discovery of this area in 1540. (The vast Coronado National Forest — comprising some 1,800,000 acres — was named after this early explorer.)

The original charter of the Old Pueblo was granted by the King of Spain in 1552. In the early 1600's Spanish Jesuits came up from Mexico to establish missions and to make Christians of the peaceful Indians. The Papago Indians who inhabited the community when it was visited in 1692 by the Spanish missionary Father Kino, called their village Stjukson (Stook-shon) which has been variously translated to mean "Dark Spring" or "at the foot of the black hill."

Father Kino founded Mission San Xavier del Bac in 1692. The Papago Indians call it "La Paloma Blanca del Desierto" which means "The White Dove of the Desert."

During this period there was constant traffic between Mexico City and Tucson as the empire-building Spaniards pushed their New World boundaries northward from Mexico City.

Mines and ranches came into being at this time, and in 1776 the Presidio of Tucson became a walled city. Some claim it was the only walled city in our nation's history. The onetime existence of a wall completely surrounding the community is the origin of Tucson's present nickname, The Old Pueblo.

In 1823 Tucson was a part of the newly-created Mexico, and served as a military outpost until it became part of the United States with the Gadsen Purchase in December, 1853.

Tucson mustered a total of sixty-eight American voters in 1861 when it elected a territorial delegate to the Confederate Congress. In 1862 Confederates from Texas marched unopposed into Tucson, but were routed three months later by the California Volunteers, who raised the flag of the United States over the Old Pueblo.

Arizona was organized as a territory in 1863. A year later John Goodwin, the first governor, declared Tucson a municipality.

When the transcontinental railroad arrived in 1881, Tucson was still a sleepy, Mexican-appearing village of a few hundred inhabitants. But by the turn of the century the Old Pueblo had become the business and supply center of a large territory and was rapidly gaining fame as a health resort where Easterners came to relax and soak up the desert sunshine.

By 1909 Tucson had grown to 7,351 population and was the largest city in Arizona. The University of Arizona had been established in Tucson in 1885.

The population more than doubled between 1950 and 1960 as greater numbers of people availed themselves of the opportunities and attractive climate to be found in Tucson.

Tucson's major attraction is probably its sunshine. In desert communities the sun shines eighty-five percent of the daylight hours. Because Tucson lies in a high valley, 2,400 feet above sea level, the climate is milder than on the desert floor; and this choice location is partly responsible for the ever-growing fame of Tucson's weather.

But such fame is not just a recent phenomenon. Arizona's fabled climate was being touted way back in the 1860's when a traveler here wrote, "The climate in winter is finer than that of Italy. It would scarcely be possible to suggest an improvement."

It is the year-round resident, rather than the winter visitor, however, who gains the special bonus of the Tucson climate. Here the sun shines about 340 days a year, with an average annual maximum temperature of eighty-two degrees. During the summer months, although daytime temperatures rise to the high nineties and more, the temperature drops at sunset, providing cool, comfortable evenings. The air is remarkably dry, and because of the low humidity even the hot weather produces little discomfort. Many find they can play golf in ninety-five degree weather without perspiring very much. And, of course, there is air conditioning everywhere.

The summer sun is often a topic of friendly exaggeration by Arizonans. The practice may have started with miners telling tall tales to travelers passing through. The same traveler who so praised Arizona's winter climate apparently never spent a summer here, perhaps because he believed the delightful exaggerations.

Today, Tucson's metropolitan area has a population approaching 500,000. All signs point to continued expansion. However, in spite of Tucson's rapid growth, it has been able to retain its Southwestern charm.

SUN CITY

Among modern cities built since the end of the Second World War, Sun City is a story all of its own for its creativity and daring. It really was the first retirement community built out in the desert in the history of this country. This was never tried before. Could this idea espoused by the famous Del Webb, work in a desert area a few miles West of the well established Phoenix, Arizona? It was novel. It was different. It became a huge success story.

In 1960 construction of a new town was started on 8,900 acres of farm land twelve miles northwest of Phoenix, Arizona, in a region where rain is infrequent, temperatures mild, and humidity among the nation's lowest.

This was not an ordinary, run-of-the-mill real estate development, but a carefully researched and master-planned community specifically designed for retirees.

In pleasant surroundings, attractive functional homes were built and recreation facilities provided to allow mature people over fifty years of age, to develop new interests and enjoy an active, rewarding way of life.

Expansion into this comparatively new industry was typical of the late Del E. Webb, who had parlayed a hammer and saw into a multi-million dollar corporation, with interests ranging from construction and land development, to hotel operations and property management.

The new community was an immediate success. During the January, 1960, premiere, thousands of visitors flocked to see what this new city had to offer America's retirees.

Not only did they find model homes, but all of the promised facilities were there, ready for inspection.

The first recreation center was complete with swimming pool, shuffleboard courts, lawn bowling green, arts and crafts studios, meeting and card rooms, and an auditorium. The first nine holes of the North Golf Course were playable and the second nine was under construction.

A motor hotel with restaurant offered accommodations for visitors, and a shopping center provided new residents with most basic services.

During opening weekend, 272 homes were sold and the new community was launched. Sales totaled 1,301 units by the end of 1960 and Sun City had a population of 2,500. By 1965 the population had reached eight thousand and it jumped to twenty-three thousand in the next five years. The first two months of 1977 showed sales of 1,277 living units, with a valuation in excess of fifty-eight million dollars. At the present time, the community sports about forty thousand residents and is the seventh largest city in Arizona.

Community facilities have kept pace with this rapid growth and Sun City now has six recreation centers.

In planning the new recreation complexes, several things are taken into consideration. Of course, population growth is one guideline and frequency of use of existing facilities points up certain needs. The other determining factor is the wishes of the residents which are determined through surveys.

Therefore, while each new recreation center has duplicated many of the existing facilities, each complex brought new things such as exercise rooms, pool and billiards, therapy baths, miniature golf, boating and fishing, tennis, ping pong, bocci ball, weaving, bowling, even a picnic area with scenic waterfall, cabanas, barbecues, and small lakes.

Sundial Center features Arizona's largest indoor swimming pool, first indoor, air conditioned shuffleboard courts, and the state's only synthetic surfaced lawn bowling green.

Bell Recreation Center features a forty thousand volume library and the community's first handball and volleyball courts.

For the green thumbers, Sun City has its agricultural gardens where gardeners can farm a 20 foot x 40 foot plot with water provided.

Residents pay a small fee per person, per year, for use of the recreation facilities.

Sun Citians have formed over four hundred clubs and organizations to take full advantage of the recreation centers.

No list would be complete without mention of the many service, fraternal, patriotic, and church organizations within the community, several of which are the largest and most active in the state.

Sun City has its own Symphony Orchestra. Cultural events also include a lecture series that presents some of the finest speakers in the nation. Many of these events are held in the Sundome, an indoor theatre with a capacity of 7,500.

The Sun Bowl, a 7,500 capacity outdoor amphitheater, has become an entertainment center for Sun Citians, as well as visitors from all over the United States.

Each winter a Celebrities Series brings some of the nation's top performing talent to Arizona. The list has included such luminaries as Liberace, Guy Lombardo, Jimmy Durante, Lawrence

Welk and his Champagne Music Makers, Roberta Peters, Roger Williams, Robert Merrill, Pete Fountain, The King Family, Patti Page, Jan Peerce, Victor Borge, and many more.

Interspersed with the headliner shows are free shows and concerts, which keep the Sun Bowl busy throughout the year.

Today Sun City sports many eighteen-hole golf courses. Sun City also has an outstanding baseball-softball stadium. During late spring and summer the Sun City Stadium becomes the home field for the Sun City Saints Girls softball team.

A trap and skeet range, small bore rifle and pistol range, and archery lists are located on the Heading Ranch, some six miles north of Sun City.

A desert picnic area for residents has also been constructed on the property, with cabanas, tables and benches, a large dance floor, barbecues, and running water.

Within a few miles of the community is Magma of Sun City, a wild game hunting preserve where sportsmen can shoot pheasant.

In keeping with Western tradition, one section of Sun City features homes on acre or larger lots, ranch-fenced corrals, optional stalls and tack rooms. Bridle paths wander through the area and there is access to desert areas nearby. Stables are also available west of Riverview Golf Course for horse owners living in the regular sections of the city.

Almost every religious denomination is represented in Sun City by the twenty-five groups meeting in their own houses of worship or community halls.

The city also has one of the finest medical facilities in the country, with the two hundred bed Walter O. Boswell Memorial Hospital. It features the modern circular patient wings with centrally located nursing stations providing visual monitoring and quick access to every room. The impressive structure is designed for expansion to four hundred rooms. Presently the hospital in 1986 has 335 beds.

The newest, Lakeview Medical Arts Center has over 100,000 sq. ft. of office space for doctors, dentists, laboratories, pharmacy, x-ray, and other medical technicians.

The community has a nursing and health care facility Sun Vally Lodge, founded by United Church of Sun City. A second "three-level" care facility has been built.

Augmenting the excellent medical services available is Sunshine Service, an organization supplied by local charities and founded by the late Rev. Duane Thistlewaite. This unique institution loans sick room equipment and supplies to residents at no cost. The Sunshine Service Warehouse has everything from hospital beds, bed pans, and exercise equipment, to crutches, splints, and wheel chairs. There is even a supply of children's beds, chairs, and playpens to help out when grandchildren are visting. Additional services include sick room and hospital visitations, locating nursing aid or companion, and even arranging emergency loans.

Sun City has two lakes, Viewpoint and Dawn. Both offer boating and fishing, but the latter is reserved to the residential homes that border it.

Viewpoint Lake, too, is partly bordered by homes, but is available to all residents through Lakeview Recreation Center.

Also bordering Viewpoint is the Lakes Club, a private dining facility with membership limited to Sun City residents and local business establishments. It features a large dining room overlooking the lake, a comfortable cocktail lounge, and a five hundred capacity banquet room.

Commercial facilities within the community include six large shopping centers which house a large percentage of Sun City's over 350 businesses and professions. Construction on a seventh shopping center will start this spring.

To accommodate visitors, King's Inn has one hundred modern rooms, swimming pool, old English dining room, large coffee shop, cocktail lounge and bar.

The area known as Sun City West took its beginnings in 1978. This new addition to Sun City also features a 7,500 seat auditorium and in 1986 had a population of about 17,000 people and it will approximate 25,000 people in a few years. Sun City West has a 14 million dollar R.H. Johnson Recreational Center on 40 acres. It is the largest senior citizen recreational center in the world.

In order to maintain the beauty and uncluttered cleanliness of the city, a fenced trailer compound has been provided for storage of campers, motor homes, boats, and trailers.

With completion of the presently master-planned 8,900 acres, it is estimated that Sun City will have a population of over 46 thousand. The Del E. Webb Development Company has approximately twelve thousand more acres adjoining Sun City on the west, for which master-planning has not been completed.

Del E. Webb was seventy-five when he passed away July 4, 1974, leaving an international building, developing, and management corporation as a lasting monument to his creative genius.

MESA — City of Mesa was founded by Mormons from Bear Lake County, Idaho, and from Salt Lake County, Utah. When the first Mormons arrived the land resembled a broad tableland from which the area derives its name. T.C. Sirrine in May 1878 deeded a section of land to form a Mormon community. The first trustees were C.R. Robson, G.W. Sirrine, and F.M. Pomeroy. The name Mesa was not accepted by the Post Office authorities because at that time there was a community in Pinal County called Mesaville. Consequently the city was first called Hayden to honor a famous Arizonian, Charles Trumbull Hayden. In what is today called the Valley of the Sun, there existed at that time two cities Hayden and Hayden's Ferry. Both were not far from each other. Because of the enormous confusion in the post office with the mail, a change in names had to be made. The city then changed its name to Zenos. Later in 1888 when the community in Mesaville in Pinal County no longer existed, the name was quickly changed to Mesa.

Thus began a tremendous history of prosperous and progressive growth of the Mormons and their church in Arizona. Mesa served as the center and the focal point and a gorgeous Temple was built there. Many other Mormon communities were founded particularly on the eastern side of the State. These hard working people with their zeal and spiritual discipline helped Arizona grow into a truly great state. No history of Arizona could be written without paying tribute to the great contributions of the Mormons in just about every dimension of society. Mesa today is a great city and in many ways it is an all American city.

Mesa is expected to have about 350,000 people in 1993.

CHAPTER 14.

The Colorado River

"The first territorial legislature convened in 1864 and created four original counties for Arizona, one of which was Yuma. It was named for its chief Indian inhabitants, the Yuma tribe, who built huge, smoky fires to induce rain and they used the word "umo" which means smoke."

Kathy Upton
Historian

If there ever was a river that controlled the destiny of a state, it was and is the Colorado. The pages of Arizona history are filled with stories about the Colorado.

The total length of the River is about 1450 miles and it has about nineteen major canyons in its course. It was so big and so powerful that the story of Arizona in many ways was the story of trying to control this river.

Arizona and California fought for years over water rights to this great bonanza.

Just before the Civil War the population of Southern Arizona increased to such an extent that the problems of feeding the people became serious. During this period of early growth, most of the food was brought from the Pacific Coast at an enormous cost. Much of the food also arrived spoiled because of the lack of refrigeration. It became apparent to all that more food could be raised if there was more agricultural land. This meant more diffusion of water resources for a greater agricultural area.

There were many elaborate schemes at that time to bring water to the desert. One of the best plans was that of a certain Doctor Oliver Wozencraft, who worked out a scheme to irrigate and colonize lands in the Imperial Valley in California which is composed of the rich alluvial soil laid down by the Colorado River. Many of his ideas spread to Arizona.

To irrigate this potentially fertile desert on both sides of the Colorado, it was necessary only to turn a part of the Colorado. For with the river riding higher than the Valley, with already established channels coursing through the desert, the water would run from the river to the valley of its own accord. Doctor Wozencraft thought of the proposition which involved a diversion of water from the Colorado River toward the west into the region drained by the Alamo River, which in turn would be distributed to points in California. From these places it could be distributed by a canal system.

To carry out Wozencraft's idea, the Federal Government was asked to grant the State of California some three million acres of land. The California Legislature approved the idea, but the U. S. Congress failed to pass the necessary legislation. The reason for Congressional disapproval was that part of the canal system to be constructed would have to be located on Mexican soil. Seventeen years later, in 1876, a survey was made to determine whether or not it would be feasible to reach the Imperial Valley without following a route through Mexico. The report of the American engineers indicated that it would be unfavorable to build the canal entirely in the U. S., and again called attention to the natural route through Mexican territory.

This news was rather discouraging to those desiring to have water supplied to the desert in a canal located throughout its entire length on U. S. soil, but efforts to develop irrigation continued, although on a smaller degree than was suggested by Wozencraft. Large scale or modern irrigation did not begin until near the end of the century, although various small enterprises were tried, as well as numerous private endeavors.

Wozencraft, born in Ohio, educated in medicine in Kentucky, first came to the Colorado desert by way of Yuma on his way to the California placers in 1849. In the desert crossing, several of his party nearly collapsed and Wozencraft set off on his own in search of water. He must have been standing on the banks of Alamo Barranca, where it crossed the boundary from Baja, California, to swing north toward the sink when he got his great idea. "It was then and there that I was first convinced of the idea of the reclamation of the desert," he later wrote.

The real history of irrigation of modern Imperial and Yuma Valleys began in 1892, when Engineer, Charles Rockwood, took preliminary steps in making large scale plans to irrigate the land with water brought from the Colorado River. As a result of Rockwood's efforts, the California Development Company was founded. The chief promoter of this firm was Colonel Ferguson. He induced J. W. Shenk, editor of the Omaha Christian Advocate, to invest $10,000 in the company. This event took place in

1899. One year later a hydraulic engineer, George Chaffey, discovered that water could be brought from the river more cheaply than had been anticipated. So he also invested in the California Development Company. In April, 1900, work was started on the canal system and the intakes in order to bring water to the firm's lands, some sixty miles west of Yuma in the Imperial Valley. The first water was delivered in June, 1901. Before long an agricultural boom had started. At the end of the fourth year, the Shenk family sold out part of their original holdings for $45,000.00, and the remaining portion brought another $40,000.00 several years later. This was quite a profit on an original investment of $10,000.00.

Like many other business enterprises, the California Development Company encountered its share of troubles. The first setback came when an agent of the U. S. Department of Agriculture began to write most discouraging articles about the soils in the Valleys. When circular number nine was issued by the Bureau of Soils in 1902, this pamphlet stated:

"Aside from the alkali, which renders the soil practically worthless, some of the land is so rough from the gullies or sand dunes that the expense of leveling it is greater than warranted by its value. In the 108,000 acres surveyed in the Imperial Valley area, twenty-seven percent are sand dunes and rough land — the remainder of the level land or fifty-one percent, contains too much alkali to be safe except for resistant crops."

In the meantime the Development Company was having internal disorder. Not only that, in 1906, the Colorado River suddenly abandoned its old-time bed to the Gulf of California and headed northwest into the Salton Sea. For the next twenty months, three unsuccessful attempts were made to get the river back into its regular channel. Finally a fourth endeavor resulted in the water's flowing again in its old course to the Gulf.

Now more and more people were coming into the vicinity around Yuma and the Imperial Valley. Most of those went south and southwest of Yuma. As additional land came under cultivation, more water was needed and after several experiments, it was decided that the best place to construct new canals from the Colorado was south of Yuma. The soil here was more desirable from a seepage standpoint, but unfortunately the site where the proposed new canals would be located, belonged to Mexico.

After much discussion about water rights and maintenance of the canal, the Mexican Government agreed to permit the construction through the desired territory. The American farmers agreed to finance all costs and supply machinery needed to dig the artificial river bed. In return they were to receive one-half of all the water which flowed through the canal. The Mexican farmers who in reality were American land owners, were to have the other fifty percent of the water going through the canal at a cost to be fixed by the Mexican Government. Later the rate proved so inadequate that, although the amount of water used there over a period of years averaged more than a fourth of the total carried, the amount of money paid to the canal owners did not meet so much as one-eighth of the expense of maintaining that portion of the project in Mexican territory.

Sometimes the Colorado River has a heavy flow of water. Then again a smaller amount comes down the river. When the rain falls high up in the mountains and the snow melts, the water comes rushing down the mountain in torrents and fills the dry creek beds.

This is what happened when the floods came to Imperial Valley in 1905-1907. The Colorado River overflowed its banks and almost destroyed the cities of Imperial Valley.

In 1906 Imperial Valley was in great danger from floods. Water was everywhere. There was no transportation except by mule or wagon, and there was constant danger of dropping into a hole or ditch as roads had been washed away. Stores were flooded and adobe buildings slowly melted away. People tried to mend the levee by putting sandbags and brush in the opening to stop the flow of water. Finally there were no more sacks to fill with sand. The merchants opened sacks of sugar, flour, etc., and dumped the contents on the counter and used these sacks for sand bags. The men worked steadily at the levee and the wives and daughters brought them food as they stood knee deep in the water. The people had no place to rest as the water was everywhere.

The people of the Valley were aware of the danger and they decided that something must be done to control the Colorado River. This disaster must not happen again. The people of the Valley must have water for irrigation, but it must be a dependable steady flow of water.

After studying the problem and gaining all the information possible, it was decided that Hoover Dam should be built to control the flow of water.

The first thing to decide was the location of the dam. The first decision was that the dam should be built in Boulder Canyon. Later it was learned that an earthquake fault was there. The engineers decided to move down stream to Black Canyon. It was first called Boulder Dam because of the location in Boulder Canyon. The name was changed to Hoover Dam in honor of Herbert Hoover, our President, at that time.

Construction of Hoover Dam started in 1931 and was completed in 1935. It was the largest dam to be built at that time. We now have some larger ones, but Hoover Dam is the highest dam in the Western Hemisphere.

Hoover Dam is the important dam for water control and regulation as far as Yuma Valley is concerned. This dam controls floods and stores water for irrigation, municipal, and industrial uses. It is also used for hydroelectric power.

The people of Yuma Valley depend upon the water stored in Lake Mead, the reservoir of Hoover Dam, to irrigate their land. This water is also used by the people of Mexico to irrigate their land. One main purpose of the dam is to supply the farmers with a steady flow of water when they need it. Before the dams were built farmers had too much water or too little or not any at all.

There is another dam in Arizona called Parker Dam, just 150 miles from Hoover Dam. As Hoover is the highest dam, Parker is the deepest. It stores water to be supplied for the people of Los Angeles and other coastal cities. It protects the people down stream from flash floods of the Bill Williams River. Work was begun on this dam in 1934, and it was finished in 1938.

Another dam was built 148 miles down stream from Parker Dam. It is called Imperial Dam. It is not used for water storage, but to divert water into the All-American Canal. Another purpose is to remove silt from the water. The silt must be taken out so that the canals will not get filled up and have to be dredged. Construction on the dam began in 1936, and six years later it was finished.

Another dam built in Arizona was the Laguna. The contract for building the dam was let to J. G. White and Company on July 6, 1905, and operation began on the 19th of the following month. In August, 1906, the contractors petitioned relief from their contract, stating that they were meeting with excessive costs. Several adjustments were made but when the contractors again petitioned for relief, the work was ordered taken over by the Reclamation Service on January 23, 1909, by force account, under the direction of the engineers of the Reclamation Service.

When finally completed, the dam was almost a mile long and raised the water ten feet from its natural elevation. The cost of the project up to 1910, including dam, levees, and canals was

$4,120,000.00, or about fifteen dollars for each acre that was expected to be irrigated in the future. A water user's association was formed and each member was to pay on the basis of number of acres irrigated. Eventually the project is to be self-liquidating. Laguna Dam has been a huge bonanza to the farming area of Arizona. Its untold benefits in dollars and cents to the average farmer's yield is uncalculable.

The waters that once brought disastrous floods to the basin of the Lower Colorado River now make these acres very fertile. Millions of people depend upon the Colorado River and its dams for hydroelectric power for industrial uses in the cities. The dams are big giants used for our protection in flood control and supply us with a steady flow of water to meet our needs.

In 1992 what is happening to the Colorado River area around Bullhead City would indeed shock the early pioneers. They could never in their wildest dreams imagine a huge gambling resort area which now occupies the Nevada side of the River. It is the city of Laughlin, Nevada, that now has about twelve gambling casinos. Bullhead City is on the Arizona side and since gambling is still not legal in Arizona, the people in the State of Arizona flock to the area in great numbers. Along with the Arizonians are thousands of Californians and others who are gradually making the spot another Las Vegas. People take advantage on the Arizona side of the free ferry ride to the Laughlin side. Laughlin is about thirty five miles from Kingman, Arizona.

Bullhead City has become the Mobile home capitol of Arizona. This is a popular way to take up residence in the gambling area. Many have a second home in this fashion while living in other homesites in California or Arizona.

CHAPTER 15.

Indians in Arizona

I have no knowledge of a case on record where a white man has been convicted and punished for defrauding an Indian. Greed and avarice on the part of the whites . . . . in other words, the almighty dollar is at the bottom of nine tenths of all our Indian trouble.

> General Crook
> Indian Fighter
> Gila country 1886

Today there is a great interest in Indian culture in this country. Television and various courses in our schools have done much to explain to the American public the interesting history and culture of the American Indian. Indian folklore is not dead and its artifacts are not antiques. On the contrary, the Indian culture in Arizona is a vital contributing force; it is a vital phenomenon of human experience existing in the midst of the dominant society.

Arizona has more Indians than any other State in the Union. Historically, Indian culture has always had to cope with its natural environment through adaptive processes that resulted in harmonies with nature, rather than processes which led to the control and change of natural environment. The Indian has been able to do this in Arizona.

Let us look at some of the notable tribes of Indians that number more than 120,000 in the State of Arizona.

THE HOPI: The Hopi live in compact villages, called Pueblos, on three mesas roughly seventy-five miles northeast of Flagstaff. Their ancestors had lived in northeastern Arizona for over two thousand years before they settled permanently on the mesas over six hundred years ago. The Hopi are well known for their craft work, particularly their carved and colorful painted wooden Kachina dolls, their fine pottery, their coiled and wicker basketry, and in recent years their overlay silver jewelry.

THE NAVAJO: The largest tribe living on the largest reservation in the United States, the Navajo are rapidly increasing in number and quickly adopting the white man's way of life. They are semi-nomadic, moving with their sheep and goats from winter to summer homes and doing some farming.

The Navajo are famous as weavers and silversmiths. The possession and display of jewelry is a significant measure of the individual's wealth; consequently quantities of "hard goods" may deck the satin skirts and velvet blouses of the women or the store-bought shirts and levis of the men.

THE APACHE: Living on the San Carlos and White Mountain Reservations, the Apache are known as the Indian Cattlemen. The men dress in typical cowboy outfits, while the women prefer long, full tiered skirts with loose over-blouses patterned after the late nineteenth century dresses. The Apache still excel at basket making.

The Apache of Arizona call themselves "inde" or "tinde" meaning the people. Until they were subdued, they were the most warlike tribe in the Southwest. Their fighting spirit was especially evident in the period from 1870 to 1900, when the encroachments of white settlers aroused them to fierce resentment. Probably the most famous of these uprisings was the series of raids waged by Geronimo.

He was born in Southern Arizona in 1829 and his Apache name was Go Khla Yeh. When Mexican soldiers attacked one of the Apache camps and killed his mother, wife, and three children, Geronimo went on the warpath. Between 1881 and 1886, he led several outbreaks, killing and plundering as he made his way into the mountains of Arizona and Mexico. He was eventually captured and sent to reservations in Florida, Alabama, and Oklahoma. He became a star attraction at the world's fair in St. Louis, Missouri, and in Buffalo, New York. He joined the Dutch Reformed Church at Fort Sill, Oklahoma, in 1903, but was expelled for gambling.

Geronimo, in 1905, rode in the inaugural parade of President Theodore Roosevelt. Later he visited the President with five other Indian chiefs.

He died at Fort Sill, on February 17, 1909.

PIMA and **PAPAGO:** Similar in cultures, the Pima (River Dwellers) and Papago (Bean People) dress in modern western styles. Most of them have become Christianized. Learning to farm with heavy machinery and large-scale agricultural planning, they are developing their economy on long range programs. The Papago also raise cattle and have fine herds. The Pima and Papago make baskets, weaving them with willow and yucca fibers.

THE PAIUTE: Living in the far northwestern part of Arizona and on reservations in four other states — California, Nevada, Utah, and Oregon — most Paiutes speak English, live and dress like the white man, and engage in cattle raising and wage work as their major source of income. The most distinctive craft created by the Paiute is the wedding basket, a coiled, shallow basket used by the Navajo Indians because of its finish and symbolic design.

THE CHEMEHUEVI: The Chemehuevi Indians are located on the Colorado River Reservation. Deserving of mention, although no longer produced, are the famous small, coiled baskets for which the Chemehuevi are well known. The baskets are simple bowls or jars with patterns usually worked in black or an occasional dark red.

THE COCOPAH: Less than a hundred in number, the Cocopah tribe lives on the lower Colorado. The majority of the tribe work on the farms of white men.

THE MOHAVE: The majority of the Mohave live on two reservations — the Fort Mohave and the Colorado River Reservations. Most of their crafts are dying out, and the Mohave women have turned from making pottery to the creation of ties, belts, capes, and purses made from glass beads.

THE HAVASUPAI: The beautiful Havasu Canyon is the reservation home of the Havasupai Indians. Relatively isolated, these people sustain themselves with farming and off-reservation-wage-work. Most of their native crafts are gone except for the conical burden baskets which the women still make.

THE HUALAPAI (or WALAPAI): Neighbors of the Havasupai, the Hualapai live in and above the canyons leading down to the Colorado River and are primarily cattlemen and lumbermen. Their basketry is well made and follows traditional designs.

THE YAVAPAI: Nomadic in nature, the Yavapai have separated into different groups, some living with Apache bands, and others at the Ft. McDowell Reservation, the Camp Verde Reservation, and the Yavapai Reservation. The Yavapai may be said to be farmers, wage workers, industrial employees, or cattle raisers, depending upon the reservation on which they live. The only native craft that survives is basketry.

THE MARICOPA: Spread between the Gila River and Salt River Reservations, the Maricopa have adopted the Pima economy and have borrowed many of the Pima crafts. Maricopa potters create "unusual-shaped" ceramic bowls, many of which have an admirable high polish and all of which have been popular commercially.

THE YUMA: Some of the Yuma Indians live in California, but many of them work in Arizona making their living by wage work. Their crafts are disappearing and only a little pottery is still made.

Arizona is Indian country. Its nineteen reservations cover nearly twenty million acres or approximately twenty-seven percent of the state. The several reservations' geography and climate range from the cool high plateau country of the Hopi and Navajo to the low arid Sonoran Desert lands of the Cocopah and Papago.

Natural resources on the reservations include coal, natural gas, copper, gemstones, sand and gravel, stone, asbestos, volcanic cinder, agricultural and grazing lands, and timber.

Scenic and recreational resources include national monuments, such as the beautiful Canyon de Chelly on the Navajo Reservation, Pipe Springs on the Kaibab Paiute Reservation, and many ancient ruins of Indian cultures of the distant past. Further examples include water sports on the Colorado River Reservation; hunting, fishing, and skiing at Sunrise Park on the Fort Apache Reservation; the Grand Canyon on the Hualapai Reservation; Kitt Peak Observatory and the historic San Xavier Mission on the Papago Reservation; and Salt River Canyon and San Carlos Lake on the San Carlos Reservation. But the Indian people and their rich culture and crafts are the reservations' greatest attraction.

The lofty mesa-top-pueblo villages of the Hopi and the remote and beautiful canyon home of the Havasupai draw many visitors. Indian craftsmen fashion the exquisite Navajo silver and turquoise jewelry, Pima and Papago basketry and Hopi pottery and hand-carved Kachina dolls.

The appeal of the Indian reservations is not limited to the tourist and outdoor recreation seeker. Business and industry have discovered the advantages of locating on the reservations.

Property tax advantages are available to businesses locating on the reservation lands. Government agencies such as the Economic Development Administration, Farmers Home Administration, Small Business Administration, Four Corners Regional Commission, and Bureau of Indian Affairs are prepared to provide to businesses a variety of services and assistance ranging from information to loans, grants, and training programs.

Several reservations including the Colorado River, Gila River, Hopi, Navajo, Papago, Salt River, and San Carlos have developed industrial parks with complete utilities, transportation facilities, and a ready labor force. Leases are available at competitive terms.

New business and industry ventures include electronics, retail trade and services, a wide range of light manufacturing, recreational and tourism facilities, agriculture and related processing, mining and utilities to name a few.

The State of Arizona does not tax Indian lands and Indian-owned property on reservations. Incomes of Indians residing on reservations are also not taxed if wholly derived from reservation sources. Indian people of Arizona are exempt from state and local sales taxes on consumer goods purchased on the reservation, unless such taxes are imposed by the tribal government. Arizona does tax the property and business transactions of non-Indians who operate on reservations and Indians who live or work off reservations.

In 1986 two Indian women entered the Arizona Women's Hall of Fame. Elected for their service and contributions to the state of Arizona, the new inductees bring to 34 the number so honored since the Hall of Fame was established in 1981 by the Arizona Women's Commission.

Viola Jimulla (1878-1906), a Yavapai tribal chieftain, who helped establish the reservation near Prescott.

Nampeyo (1860-1942), a Hopi potter and archaeologist known in the Indian art world as "the Old Lady," and credited with reviving the art of fine pottery making.

Almost all Indian tribes in Arizona now have gambling as a legal entity on their reservations. The prosperous casinos are popular recreational centers. The lucrative profits from many gambling casinos enhance the educational and social life of the Indian tribes.

CHAPTER 16.

Bisbee Deportation

The main reason why there is so much crime among our young people in Arizona and in our country, is because most mothers are working. They are not at home to take care of the children. There is no substitute for mothers.

Barry Goldwater
Interview with author
January 1994

On June 26, 1917, a strike was called in Bisbee, which was to be probably the most famous strike in all of Arizona history. Around two thousand miners walked off their jobs at three copper companies which were in operation at that time. They were the Copper Queen Division of Phelps Dodge Corporation, the Calumet and Arizona Mining Company and the Shattuck Arizona Mining Company.

Two Labor Unions were involved. One was the International Union of Mine, Mill and Smelter Workers and the other was the International Workers of the World's Metal, Mine Workers Industrial Union, better known as the Wobblies. The latter was usually allied to Communist ideology and it had a reputation at that time for agitating against capitalistic enterprises. The Wobblies brought on the strike and had some help from the other union. At that time unions were not too particular as to what methods were used to obtain some of their objectives. And the Wobblies in particular had become Public Enemy Number One in the minds of most people.

Because of the war, there was a great demand for copper and Bisbee had attracted a number of workers who were not ideal citizens. There was the usual aura of suspicion about events and people that always seems to abound during perilous times in our history.

Out of nowhere a special task force was organized called the Workmen's Loyalty League. These were the good guys who decided that enough was enough. They numbered about two thousand and they were well organized Their enemies were the strikers and the Wobblies in particular.

On July 12, 1917, starting early in the morning, Bisbee started a roundup of the strikers in a fashion unprecedented in our nation's history. The deputized Loyalty League in Army style form, rounded up about 1,186 bad guys from all parts of Bisbee. They were placed in cattle cars by force and their destination was to be New Mexico.

To make sure that federal and state authorities would not interfere, all telegraph and telephone communications were cut off.

The train left in the afternoon on that memorable day of July 12, 1917, in what was to be called in history, the "Wobbly Special." Riding on top of the cars were about two hundred heavily armed guards, all members of the Loyalty League.

This notorious train was to arrive that same day in Columbus, New Mexico, at nearly midnight. In Columbus there was a problem. Officials at that city refused to allow the prisoners to disembark. In desperation the train moved about 15 miles toward the Arizona border to a little village in New Mexico, called Hermanas. There the prisoners were told to scatter to the four winds and were warned never to enter Bisbee because the threat of death would hang over them. A. U.S. Army calvary unit was to arrive some hours later to escort the men to a tent stockade where they were given provisions and some protection against the heat of the day. The Army did not consider the men to be prisoners and, of course, they were allowed to go free. Apparently the Army took good care of the men, for it was not until September did the last group leave and only after the Army began a program of giving them half rations.

This whole incident was to be called in the annals of Arizona history, the Bisbee Deportation. It was to eventually obtain world wide publicity and many wondered about justice in the Wild West.

The Wobblies actually increased their memberships throughout the U. S. because of what happened in Bisbee. President Wilson created a special commission to be sent to Bisbee to investigate the whole matter. One of the members of the commission was Felix Frankfurter who was to later become a Justice of the Supreme Court. The Arizona Governor at that time, Thomas E. Campbell, and his State Attorney, Wiley E. Jones, personally investigated.

The Wobblies continued to agitate at mining camps other than Bisbee. The latter incident seemed to spur them on to greater organization. It must be reported that they were similarly deported in smaller numbers from Jerome and from Globe. However, these incidents were to never gain the notoriety of the famous Bisbee Deportation.

To this day there are divisions of thought as to whether the Bisbee Deportation was right or wrong. One thing is certain, Bisbee was put on the map and receives national attention to this day over the famous strike.

It is to be noted that the Bisbee Deportation incident was directed by Cochise County Sheriff Harry Wheeler. But he was a mere pawn in the political and economic, copper dynasties run by copper barons and politicians who profited handsomely from the mine revenues. Phelps Dodge orchestrated the whole affair and even distributed guns and ammunition to the posse. In the long drawn out affair between management and labor, the former was helped to a great degree by the special friendship that existed between President Woodrow Wilson and Cleveland H. Dodge, a director of Phelps Dodge. Also in the Governor's race of 1916, Thomas Campbell, a Republican and very pro-management, defeated George W.P. Hunt, whose platform favored unions. Then there was the news media at that time that whipped up sentiment against the unions.

Absentee owned mines prospered at Bisbee, Jerome, Globe-Miami and at Clifton-Morenci. Mexican workers were paid half of what others earned. It is also to be noted that Walter Douglas became President of the American Mining Congress. He drew other owners to help in the fight to ruin the unions. History can ask this question at the time: Was the deck stacked against the miners and their unions?

CHAPTER 17.

The Famous Yuma Crossing

"Distance often give erroneous interpretation, as well as enchantment. We think that this is somewhat the case with Yuma. It is not an Indian village; though an Indian village exists contiguous to it, and a full representation of the old Yuma tribes constitute an equal half of its daily population. Blanketed and half nude Indians associate as intimately with the white (what few there are here) as do the Mexicans themselves. The town itself, is strictly of Mexican origin, and savors of all the looseness and primitiveness characteristic of the smaller, out of the way towns in the Republic of Mexico. One sees a mass of one story buildings, built of adobe, and roofed with mud... Some whitewashed and with a clear appearance; while others as embodiment of the filth of the area."

E. Conklin
in Picturesque Arizona, 1878

Of all the cities and areas in the United States, very few have played such a powerful role in history as the Yuma Crossing. Not only is Yuma, Arizona, one of our oldest cities, but it has had a very historical impact on the history of the Southwest. It was the meeting place of the Gila and Colorado Rivers. All movement going into Southern California and for that matter the whole of the Southwest, went through Yuma and its famous Crossing.

In 1826 Lieutenant R. W. H. Hardy, of the British Navy, traveling in Mexico, chartered the 25-ton schooner Bruja (Sea Witch) in Guaymas, Mexico, and came to the Yuma Crossing.

In 1827 Sylvester and James Ohio Pattie, two fur trappers, visited Yuma and went south to the Gulf of California. James Ohio Pattie's, "Personal Narrative," remains to this day as a wonderful little book concerning the story of early trade in the Southwest.

During 1825 and 1826, the Patties trapped on the Gila and operated copper mines at Santa Rita. The younger Pattie discovered a route from New Mexico to the eastern boundary of California. He explored much of the Colorado River (including the Grand Canyon), traversed the Central Rocky Mountain region as far north as the Yellowstone and the Platte, and followed the Arkansas to the south, where he crossed to the Rio Grande which brought him to Santa Fe, New Mexico. At one time while in California with a vaccine which his father had discovered, he helped vaccinate about 22,000 persons against a ravaging epidemic of smallpox. In the words of Reuben Gold Thwaites, "brave, honest, God-fearing, vigorous in mind and body, dependent on their own resources, the Patties belonged to that class of Americans who conquered the wilderness and pushed the frontier westward."

With the advent of the war with Mexico in 1846, the Yuma Crossing, still under the flag of Mexico, had tremendous strategic importance.

There were two objectives in the overall policy of President Polk. One was to win the northern provinces of Mexico. On the day war was declared against Mexico, he told the cabinet: "In making peace with our adversary, we shall acquire California, New Mexico, and other further territory, as an indemnity for this war, if we can." The second objective was to end the struggle quickly.

In keeping with this plan, the "Army of the West," was formed with the aim of winning California and New Mexico. Colonel Stephen W. Kearny assembled this force at Ft. Leavenworth on the Missouri River in the spring of 1846. He recruited three hundred regular dragoons, a thousand Missouri frontiersmen, five hundred Mormon youths who volunteered from the camp at Council Bluffs, Iowa, where Brigham Young was preparing to lead his people westward, and enough miscellaneous recruits to bring the total to 2,700 men.

While in Santa Fe, New Mexico, Kearny eventually divided his army into three parts and each had a mission. One of these armies numbering about three hundred men along with the Colonel, started for California and passed through Yuma. Along the way, they met Kit Carson, bearing the welcome news that California was already won.

Kearny then sent a large segment of his army back to Santa Fe. He enlisted the aid of Carson to help him trek the remaining miles to California with about one hundred men.

Following Kearny across the plains came the so-called Mormon Battalion, which had enlisted in the U. S. Army for one year. This energetic group was under the command of Philip St. George Cooke. They did not take the same route as Kearny's Battalion. They passed through Yuma several months behind him. The long 1,400 mile wagon route taken by Lt. Col. Cooke and his men, was to become famous over the years. As Cooke wrote in his report, "marching half naked and half fed, and living upon wild animals, we have discovered and made a road of great value to our country. History may be searched in vain for an equal march of infantry." They arrived in San Diego in January, 1847.

For many years, the Indians in the Yuma area had a profitable business of helping people across the wild Colorado. With the discovery of gold in California, the increase in passengers made it necessary for a ferry service to operate and Lieutenant Cave J. Coutts was the first ferry master. He operated the ferry in the late fall of 1849. He was a soldier in command of an escort attached to the boundary surveyor team. On the first of November, 1849, a flatboat which had made the voyage down the Gila from the Pima villages with a Mr. Howard and family and two men, arrived at the surveyor's camp. The lieutenant immediately purchased the flatboat and used it as a ferry during the remainder of his stay. This was the beginning of the ferry business in the Yuma area.

The year 1849 was a memorable one in the history of the Yuma Crossing. Thousands of gold seekers heading for the rich lodes in California passed through this area. Some historians claimed that as many as 60,000 miners or prospectors went through the Yuma Crossing in a 12-month period.

With the end of the war with Mexico in 1848, and the signing of the Treaty of Guadalupe Hidalgo, many problems faced the government in Washington. One was the fact that many areas in the new lands of New Mexico and California did not have proper markings or any accurate maps. Thus, the U. S. Government sent several survey teams into this new territory, many of which passed through Yuma.

One of the first survey teams came in 1851, led by Captain Lorenzo Sitgreaves with a party of infantrymen. He crossed the area of the 35th parallel and made a careful examination of the land which some years later became the route of the Santa Fe Railroad.

In 1853 Lieutenant Amiel Whipple, a veteran of the Boundary Survey, came into the Yuma area with a group of topographical engineers.

While Whipple was locating passengers to the San Francisco Mountains, another expedition under Lieutenant John G. Parke, arrived in Yuma for topographical study.

The majority of the early writings about the vicinity at the junction of the rivers indicate that there were three settlements on the Arizona side of the Colorado River, all within a distance of a mile or so. One of these became known as Colorado City, and consisted of only one adobe building that was used as a customs' house. A short distance away was another small settlement called Arizona City, which had half a dozen adobe buildings, including two stores, two saloons and a post office. The third settlement was located at the ferry one mile below the junction. Here were found two stores, two blacksmith shops, a hotel, several houses, and a stage station.

Within the seven years between 1854 and 1861, the three settlements evolved into what is Yuma today, although it was not designated officially as such until a bill was passed by the 7th Arizona Legislature in January, 1873, changing the name from Arizona City to Yuma.

The town site that had been laid out by the Poston Party in 1854, was duly registered in the records of San Diego County. For some time, Yumans paid their taxes to the tax collector from San Diego.

The first mail route from the Pacific coast was the same one which had been used by the herdsmen. Mail eastbound from California started from San Diego in October, 1857. Stages were not used until supply depots had been established along the road. Before this was done, the mail was carried in saddle bags. To take the letters east from Yuma to Tucson required three days and two nights in a buckboard. Horses were changed every 15 miles, and as a rule there was at least one passenger. The greatest Apache danger came in the stretch of desert between Oatman Flats 90 miles east of Yuma, and Picacho Hill near Tucson. The following was taken from the *San Diego Herald* for November 21, 1857, describing the stage route from that city east:

> "Stage fares from San Diego are as follows: To Yuma, $35.00; to Tucson, $75.00; to El Paso, $120.00; to San Antonio, $150.00 including meals. Each man proposing to go, should provide himself with a rifle and 100 cartridges; a Colt's revolver and two pounds of balls, knife, and a sheathe; a pair of thick boots and woolen pants ... a soldier's overcoat ... Such money as he takes should be in silver and small gold."

In September, 1858, John Butterfield from New York, signed a six-year contract to carry the mail through from St. Louis to San Francisco, twice weekly at $600,000 a year. The Butterfield line which afterward became the Overland Mail Company, represented the height in stage coach efficiency. It had 100 Concord coaches, 1,000 horses, 500 mules and 750 employees, and it operated between San Francisco and Tipton, Missouri, at the western end of the Missouri Pacific Railroad. The contract with the government required the line to make the 2,759 mile trip in 25 days; but the usual time was 23, and once, it was cut down to 16 days. Although it provided the best service possible, the Butterfield was noted for more speed than comfort. The heavy Concord coaches were drawn by teams of four broncos, which were changed at stations scattered along the route. There was an exciting interval of bucking and stampeding when a fresh team was harnessed, and throughout the journey the coach often lurched dangerously on and off the road.

Eventually, the Civil War disrupted means of communication in the Southwest and transportation in Arizona suffered a setback from which it was long in recovering. Some of the stock and other property of the Butterfield Line was confiscated by the Confederates in Texas in 1861, and the lack of military protection in Arizona against the Indians and road agents was an added reason for discounting the service. During the 1860's and early 1870's, there were a few stagecoach and horseback mail lines operating in Arizona. And there were steamboats on the Colorado River, but in the main, Arizona was virtually cut off from adequate communication with the outside world. There was little intercourse even between points within the territory during this period.

Eighteen hundred and fifty-eight and fifty-nine were important years in the Yuma area. They brought permanent residents, a new steamer, and the discovery of gold on the Gila.

Many Americans and Mexicans who returned from California were frustrated because they did not find gold, and they stopped along the areas of the Yuma Crossing and hunted for the rich, yellow lode.

Jacob Snively, a man from Texas, found the dust about eighteen miles above Fort Yuma. News spread all over the United States and for a while, the Yuma area was a repetition of the California Gold strike. The area where gold was found by Snively became Gila City, and about a thousand people suddenly appeared to make the City a new hub of activity. The gold rush was on. The San Francisco Chronicle in 1853 had this to report:

"It appears from what I can learn that these mines are situated on the Gila, about eighteen miles from Fort Yuma, on the north bank, northwest from Yuma itself. By the river, it is about forty miles from the diggin's. There is a flat bottom or overflowed sand intervening between the river and the mountains, and the gold is found in the gulches and canyons leading down from the mountains into the Gila. The workmen here and all around are busily engaged in making tools and other appliances used for mining purposes. One wagon load of implements has already departed and it is supposed the miners have been supplied with the necessary instruments — such as picks, shovels, rockers, etc. The climate and temperature is represented to be similar to that of the hottest parts of California. Mr. White, who owns a "rancho" on the Gila, some fifty miles about Fort Yuma, states that there are eleven immigrant families living there at present and some forty or fifty miners at work; and those who worked steadily were averaging over five dollars a day. He further stated that Mr. Riddle had worked in the mines one month and had taken out five hundred dollars. Mr. Birch, who has been working there two months, has taken out eight hundred dollars. Mr. Johnson, who has worked nearly a month, has taken out $250. The dirt after being dug out of the face of the hills and in the gulches is packed to the river, and washed, which renders mining a very laborious experience and tedious way of getting rich. As to the extent of the diggins, Mr. White estimates that they extend sixteen miles up and down, on both sides of the river."

However, the gold strike did not last long. There was no rich discovery of any kind. The settlement soon vanished and Gila City became a ghost town.

In 1862 Arizona City suffered a severe flood. At this time the Gila River overflowed her banks to such an extent, that water stood twenty feet deep on a ranch in the bottom lands just above the town. The town virtually had to be rebuilt again. This was one of many disasters that the future area of Yuma was to suffer.

In 1863 Mineral City was founded. The year is also important for the Castle Dome mines were discovered and Arizona became a Territory.

In 1864 Yuma County was laid out with La Paz as the county seat and it was in this year, that the first Pony Express came to Yuma. But in 1867, Yuma, as we know it, began to mature as a site. Permanent homes replaced huts; there were streets and new stores. Mexicans came from Sonora and many came from California. The rich soil near the river produced abundant crops. Wagon factories were established to take care of the overland freighters.

In 1866 the Post Office was established and the Arizona Vigilantes organized.

In 1870, Arizona City, was made the County seat of Yuma County. When the San Diego tax collector arrived in the following fall, there was trouble. When he demanded that the taxes be paid in gold coin, an excited citizen swore out a warrant charging the man with an attempt to collect money under false pretenses. Fortunately for him, some of the more calm citizens deposited bail for his temporary release to appear in court.

Immediately the troubled man wrote to San Diego to inquire what action he should take. His friends advised him to leave the place under cover of darkness. No time was lost in doing this, and his bondsmen were left in a bad state of mind. All of them declared they would never pay another cent to the San Diego authorities, and from that time on the citizens of Yuma have carried out their threat. History seems to record the fact that the people of Yuma always wanted to be identified with the area known as Arizona.

Political organization followed on the heels of settlement in the West. After the admission of Kansas as a state in 1861, the remaining territories of Washington, New Mexico, Utah and Nebraska were divided into smaller and more convenient units. By the close of the sixties territorial governments were in operation in the new provinces of Nevada, Colorado, Dakota, Arizona, Idaho, Montana, and Wyoming. The political map of the United States was complete except for the division of the Dakotas and the organization of the Indian Territory, the future Oklahoma.

Shortly after the gold and silver seekers had built a mineral empire, another great economic province began to take shape in the last frontier. The cattle kingdom was born on the Great Plains, its imperial boundaries stretching from the plains of Kansas to California and from Texas to Canada. Like the mining domain, it had a brief and brilliant existence, from approximately 1865 to 1885, and during the period, it influenced materially the course of national development, and added another colorful chapter to the record of the area now known as Arizona and California.

The rise of the cattle kingdom was directly related to the expanding industrial society of urban America. The multitude of new metropolitan centers created a new, huge market for meat and other foods, and this was particularly true of California. Hence, the business of herding cattle from Texas to California by way of Yuma came into existence.

This venture of herding animals all the way from the Rio Grande region to the markets on the Pacific Coast started about 1847. The route followed was the famous old trail from the East which crossed the Rio Grande River near El Paso, and traversed the southern edge of both New Mexico and Arizona in a general westerly course, until reaching the boundary between them, some two hundred miles, and thence in the same general direction several hundred miles to Tucson. The trail turned north here for about ninety miles to the Pima Indian villages on the Gila River, then down the southern side of this stream to the Colorado River at Yuma. Thus, thousands of cattle and many cowboys came to the Yuma Crossing.

Many cattlemen took the trail to California for the profits were exceedingly large after the Mexican War. The business for ferrying cattle across the water at the junction became so profitable that several concerns entered the field. If the cattlemen were fortunate enough to arrive when the water happened to be at a low stage, the animals waded or swam to the other bank. This would result in quite a saving.

Various factors enabled the cattle industry to spread over the West — the suppression of the Indians, the elimination of the buffalo, the laxity of the land laws — but the most important were the open range and railroads. The open range afforded a huge area for the herds to move about unrestricted. The railroads gave the cattle kingdom access to markets and thus brought it into being. In ancestry however, the cattle industry was Mexican and Texan. Long before the Americans came to the Yuma Crossing, Mexican ranchers and vaqueros had developed the techniques and tools employed later by the cattlemen and cowboys of the West.

Slowly but surely, Arizona City (Yuma) began to grow. One of the most important families to come here was the Contreras family. Before Mrs. Contreras died, she had brought twenty-one children into the world.

Francisco Contreras and wife, Delores, went to California from Sonora, Mexico, in 1833. After living in that state for twenty-five years, they came back to the junction of the Gila and Colorado for farming and to prospect for gold. At the time of their arrival, the family consisted of eight or nine children in addition to mother and father. They settled about ten miles north of Fort Yuma on the west bank of the Colorado and called the place El

Colorado. The site happened to be near the ruins of San Dionisio Mission which had been destroyed a few years after the middle of the 18th century.

A few days after the settlement had been made, one son, Antonio, returned to Los Angeles to induce a former friend to come back with him to establish a general merchandise store. The other members of the family started to prospect for gold. And gold they did find.

Eventually the family opened a general merchandise store and settled in Laguna, a new mining site, to sell their supplies to the many gold seekers coming from Altar, Sonora, Los Angeles, and San Bernardino.

The gold excitement began to subside in about six years. By that time many people had started to farm and raise cattle on both sides of the Colorado. This was the period when the Contreras family moved from Laguna and Colorado Camp to the town site of Yuma, which was soon a flourishing village. At first only temporary huts of sticks and mud were erected, but within the ensuing year all the residents began to construct adobe houses. This all took place in 1867, after the territorial government had made a survey of the Yuma site.

In 1864, the United States Government established Yuma depot. The buildings erected were good, substantial structures, and within two weeks after completion, were filled with provisions, camp equipment and military stores of every description.

The Commissary building, two hundred feet in length, fronted on the river, had a track run through the center of the structure. The supplies were unloaded from the steamboats onto cars and hauled either to store rooms, or right through the Commissary building to the south end, where from a high platform they were put aboard the immense freight wagons which were in waiting.

The Yuma depot was the supply station for Southern Utah and Nevada, Arizona, New Mexico and Western Texas. The freight was transported from here by wagons which required from sixteen to twenty miles to haul them. Armed escorts accompanied the freight trains, to protect them against the bloodthirsty and thieving Apache, but very often, in spite of all care and strategy, the red-handed savage would succeed in overpowering the freighters, killing all they could, robbing the wagons and taking the horses and mules. The old wagon and stage roads through

Arizona were the scenes of many a terrible and bloody struggle, between the government freighters and the muderous Apache, whose hand was always ready to rob and kill.

Major William B. Hooper was the first Quartermaster in charge of Yuma Depot. He afterwards founded the great mercantile house of Hooper and Company, which firm was eventually succeeded by James M. Barney and Company. Major Hooper is spoken of yet by "old timers" here as a true, generous, conscientious officer and gentleman.

Three years after being built, Yuma Depot was destroyed by fire and government loss was said to exceed the sum of five hundred thousand dollars. A Court of Inquiry was convened, and it was found that the fire was caused by some of the boys smoking cigarettes. Captain George W. Hughes was the officer in charge at the time of the conflagration.

The fire took place during the great flood of 1867, and the U. S. wagon master, Tom Hayes, who was dispatched to send a telegram to San Diego, had to swim several sloughs with his horse before he reached the telegraph office. The town of Yuma at that time was not blessed with telegraph service.

Within a few weeks after the fire, a large force of carpenters and masons were put to work, and Yuma Depot was rebuilt in "finer style" than ever. During the years following several officers of the army who since have become quite noted, were in command of the depot. Among this number may be named Generals A. G. Rockwell, A. B. D. Lee and C. E. Dandy. The last officer in charge was Colonel Strang who succeeded Major J. H. Lord. The government finally abandoned the place in 1880, removing the fine pump, tools, machinery and supplies to Fort Lowell.

A few of the buildings are now temporarily occupied by persons whose homes were washed away in the late flood.

The steady swish of the red waters of the swift-flowing Colorado are still heard about the old place; the same bright skies are above, but one stir, excitement and hum of the business has been stilled apparently forever, and Old Yuma seems to be sleeping the sleep of eternity.

In 1870, the county seat moved to Arizona City (Yuma). All county files and office equipment were floated down the Colorado River by boat. During this year the first bank also was established.

In 1875, Yuma had developed into a settled community. No longer was it just a place in which to rest before continuing on a journey. Many of the former travelers returned to settle here.

Yuma experienced a progressive growth from 1900 to the era of the First World War. More people began to come into the city and surrounding territory as soon as the Yuma Reclamation Project became a reality. After years of fighting the water question, it appeared that some of the answers to a better distribution of water had been found. People with surplus funds were encouraged to invest their money in irrigation enterprises when water from the Colorado and Gila Rivers became obtainable at reasonable rates.

In January 1910, a Los Angeles architect by the name R. B. Young, was chosen to supervise the construction of the new courthouse and jail. A great deal of wrangling and politics had preceded the final decision in the construction of the county courthouse. Many Yumans wanted it built on Prison Hill. Finally, two contractors, John Wadin and Charles Olcester, started and completed the long delayed courthouse and jail.

The authorities ran into less trouble when they built several new schoolhouses. Before 1908 there was a grammar school on Main Street, and during this year one was built on Second Avenue at a cost of $45,000. The cost of operating these institutions at the time was about $25,000 a year. The major part of the expenditures was used to pay teachers salaries, which ranged from seventy-five to ninety dollars a month.

The citizens had enough foresight to purchase a high school site in 1909. During that year the mayor, Mr. J. H. Shanssey, sold at public auction block number 121 of the city plat to the board of trustees of the Union High School for the sum of $1,000. In 1912, bonds for $60,000 were sold and by the fall of 1914, the new Union High School was ready for occupancy. This building is located on the mesa between Fourth and Fifth Streets and Fifth and Sixth Avenues.

In addition to the structures described above, a new Elks' Hall was built at a cost of $20,000. It too, is located on the higher ground above the city.

The banks also came in for their share of expansion after 1900. The Yuma National Bank was granted a charter by the comptroller of the currency on December 14, 1909, and was open for business by January of the new year. This bank at first occupied office space which had been used by the Yuma Title Abstract and Trust Company on Second Street. Four months after it opened its door, there was a reorganization, and a month after that the firm consolidated with the Farmers and Merchants Bank under the name of the Yuma National Bank.

At the same time the banking facilities were moved from Second Street to the quarters occupied by the Farmers and Merchants Bank. In 1916 the concern moved to their new home at the corner of Main and Second Street.

The First National Bank also had a healthy growth. It too began to expand after the turn of the century until in 1913, the capital had increased from $50,000 to $100,000. This institution and the Yuma National Bank were important factors in financing the business life not only of the city of Yuma, but of the farming and mining activities in the adjoining territory as well.

A comparison of Yuma as it was in 1872 with the Yuma of 1913, reveals that only about five of the Americans who had lived there at that early date still remained 41 years later. Main Street was the same but only two houses were left in 1913. Gila Street also remained the same as far as location, but not one original house was discernible by that year. Madison Avenue from Second Street to Third coincided with the streets of 1913. On or near Madison Avenue were found 9 houses that had been built by 1872, although it was hard to recognize them at the turn of the century. In the section beginning with First Avenue extending toward the west and south, not a single home could be found that had been there in 1872. By 1913 the mesa had become the residential district of the city. Before this date the locality had been the favorite resort for horseback riding and driving, and the site of a race track.

A few years after the first decade of the 20th century the automobile began to appear in Yuma in ever-increasing numbers. On January 16, 1913, Mr. W. M. Winn received his first car load of Fords direct from the factory. The coming of so many automobiles brought about demands for a new highway bridge across the Colorado River. Consequently, by February the U. S. Government had passed a measure matching the Arizona legislature's $25,000 appropriation. It was now up to California to vote a similar amount in order to construct the proposed bridge. Since the lawmakers were slow in obtaining the money, the people in California raised the necessary money through donations.

In April, 1915, the job was completed and a great celebration was undertaken. On the 11th of the month 25 automobiles passed over the new structure on their way to Holtville, California.

The coming of the automobile also created a demand for paved highways. The first large project in Yuma was the Main Street paving job. The contract was let to the O. and C. Construction Company in November, 1916, and the work was completed by March, 1917.

Today Yuma has a population of about 55,000 and it has a booming tourist trade. The Mexican free port city of San Luis Rio Colorado is located 14 miles southwest of Yuma.

Four highly productive irrigated farming areas totaling nearly 281,885 acres have made Yuma a principal agricultural trade center. A growing livestock industry is capable of feeding some 250,000 cattle in pen operations annually. It has a very visible and gigantic citrus business and its reputation is known worldwide.

Arizona Western College, a two year Junior College, is located in Yuma. Opened in 1963, the College is divided into the liberal arts and science programs which enable students to transfer to the upper division of universities and a vocation-technical program is also available, including courses in electronics and data processing. The author was on its very first faculty.

Visitor attractions in and around Yuma include the Old Territorial Prison, Fort Yuma and 16th century Saint Thomas Mission across the river. Fishing, water skiing and swimming at lakes along the Colorado River are attractive sports to residents and tourists alike.

CHAPTER 18.

Higher Education in Arizona

President Ulysses S. Grant was very interested in the cause of the American Indian. He created a famous peace policy for dealing with the Indians. The commanding general of the Department of Arizona was given orders henceforth to treat the Apaches in 1871 with "moral persuasion and kindness, looking forward to their Christianization," and to set up "feeding stations" where the Indians could come for rations while awaiting the establishment of permanent reservations.

Pat Sievers
Historian

Three State Universities dominate higher education in Arizona. Although the three are autonomous, all report to the same Board of Regents. The Regents, in turn, are responsible to the Legislature.

Arizona State University is located in Tempe, Arizona. The oldest school in the state, Arizona State, is also the largest in terms of enrollment. Established in 1885 as the Arizona Territorial Normal School, it later became Arizona State College and in 1958, achieved university status. Like the other state universities, Arizona State is governed by the Board of Regents. It has about 40,000 students.

Arizona State University is organized into the Colleges of Liberal Arts, Architecture, Business Administration, Education, Engineering Sciences, Fine Arts, Law and Nursing, a Graduate School of Social Service Administration, Summer Sessions and University Extension, a Graduate College, and fifty-two departments of instruction. The departments are responsible for the major teaching, research and service programs of the University, aided by the University libraries, museums, centers, and other services.

The University offers eight Bachelor's degrees covering nearly all fields, fifteen Masters degrees, the Ph.D. in thirteen fields, Doctor of Business Administration degree, Doctor of Education degree, and the Juris Doctor degree in the College of Law.

Arizona State University is accredited by the North Central Association of Colleges and Secondary Schools. Professional programs in the various colleges, schools, divisions and departments are accredited by the corresponding national bodies. Arizona State University is a member of the National Association of State Universities and Land-Grant Colleges, the International Association of Universities, and is affiliated with the American Council on Education and other international national and regional associations.

The University has a great reputation in the field of athletics. This is particularly true of its football, track, and baseball programs.

Northern Arizona University is located in Flagstaff, Arizona. Northern Arizona Normal School enrolled its first students in September, 1899. Over the years, the school grew to become successively, a teacher's college, a state college, and then in 1966, a state university. From a modest beginning, Northern Arizona has grown in size to an enrollment of almost 14,000 students.

Graduate courses have been offered since the 1930's and now the school offers a Master's degree in seven fields and both an Ed.D. and the Ph.D. Perhaps the best known of its departments are those of Forestry and of Anthropology, but NAU offers a broad and deep array of courses in many areas, and especially in the various fields of education.

Historically, the University has regarded itself as a school which allows students to retain their individuality, as a "personal university" so to speak. Although expanded growth has made this more difficult, it strives still to retain this trait.

The University of Arizona is located in Tucson, Arizona. It was established as a Land-Grant College in 1885, but its first classes were not held until 1891. For twenty years the school advanced slowly, but then statehood and an increasing population provided the impetus for a decade of rapid expansion. New schools and colleges were created and old ones reorganized; in these later years new research, teaching and service divisions such as the Arizona Bureau of Mines and the Laboratory of Tree Ring Research were added. At present the University is made up of fourteen colleges, four additional teaching departments, and over twenty research and special public service units.

Besides the numerous fields in which the undergraduate may major, a Master's degree can be obtained in 105 different subjects; and in sixty-five of these disciplines a Doctorate may be achieved. The newly organized College of Medicine began conferring the M. D. in May, 1971.

In addition to having several departments, most notably Anthropology and Astronomy, with an international reputation, the University possesses in the University Library and the many smaller libraries on campus, the largest academic library collection in the Southwest, with holdings approaching the two million mark. The school has about 37,000 students.

There is no Dental School in Arizona nor is there a veterinarian program for students. In 1992 severe budget problems are facing the Presidents of the three universities because of the recession. Northern Arizona University already has limited the number of students who may enter and the other two universities are moving in that direction in the near future. However, economic constraints do not hinder the head football coach at Arizona State University from obtaining a payment of about 500,000 dollars a year when all the perks are put together. Arizona State is noted for its fine athletic programs and its huge football stadium which seats about 76,000.

Grand Canyon University is one of the bigger, private schools in Arizona. It provides a Christian atmosphere where religious issues are discussed and the University encourages a conservative value system. The college was chartered on August 1, 1949, in Prescott, Arizona, where it was at first a school for preachers. After two years it moved to Phoenix on a 70 acre tract where it presently is. Today it is known for its teacher education program, sciences, nursing, business, music and the arts. In May of 1984, the College trustees voted for a transition to university status. It officially became a university in 1989 on its 40th anniversary. The university is accredited by the North Central Association of Colleges and Schools. It is considered to be one of the finest Christian Universities in the Southwest.

CHAPTER 19.

The Story of Air Conditioning in Arizona

"The distinctive feature of small republics is permanence; that of large republics varies, but always with a tendency towards empire. Almost all small republics have had long lives. Among the larger republics, only Rome lasted for several centuries, for its capital was a republic.

Simon Bolivar, 1816

What would Arizona be like without air conditioning and the evaporative cooler? They changed the social and economic life of the torrid West. They made the desert boom. We shall attempt to summarize the highlights of this development.

Some form of air cooling for mankind as a whole is really nothing new. The science of cooling was known to the world for a long time. The author visited the ruins of the ancient city of Pompeii and noticed a primitive form of air-conditioning in the homes.

Early uses of evaporating cooling are the canvas covered canteens for soldiers' drinking water, the canvas desert water bags used widely in the United States, and the "ollas" or porous water jars, of the American Indians and Mexicans. Then there was the system where vertical cloth strips hung in open windward windows, kept wet by absorption from troughs on the sill.

There was no real inventor of the science of air conditioning in the State of Arizona. There were many who tried all kinds of mechanisms to keep cool. In the hot parts of the desert, natives simply slept outside. With the advent of ice in the 1880's, Arizonans many times would put their sheets in a bucket of ice. Then several times during the night they would spread them over the bed to keep cool.

Eventually with the birth of electricity, electric fans made their debut. Many were rather crude and the electricity was not always discharging enough power in the remote areas of the desert and many were not too effective. Householders assisted their wet cloth-hung-windows with electric fans.

In cooling the desert in Arizona, history seems to record three advanced systems. First there was the iceless refrigerator, then the evaporative cooler and finally the air condition unit. The latter two units are still very much in use today.

The advent of the iceless refrigerator took birth probably just before World War One in Arizona. It was a box covered with burlap sacking. Atop was a metal tank, hand filled with water, which dripped down around the box. The breezes evaporated the water and brought enough cool air to the box to prevent butter from melting.

The Marco Polo of evaporative coolers in the state of Arizona, was Oscar Palmer who lived in Paradise Valley. He was the pioneer who paved the way in this field.

In the summer of 1977, I had the privilege of talking to Oscar. He was a young seventy eight years, and his eyes lit up when we talked about his passion, the evaporative cooler.

His life time expertise in this field of cooling towers, forced draft towers, and evaporative coolers, started with his Dad in a shop at 242 West Washington Street in Phoenix. The shop made troughs for sheep ranches and storage tanks for water. They also made the famous iceless refrigerators which were very popular in Arizona. Oscar recalls that they sometimes waited for a cash customer to come in, so that he and his father might buy dinner. A favorite at that time was a ten cent pie and a bottle of milk for the two of them.

Next came a move to 320 West Washington Street. The rags to riches story began to accelerate. Oscar first developed with his Dad a radiator for automobiles so they would not overheat in the desert. The auto companies in Detroit just could not cope with this problem in Arizona. He is famous for his patent on the "Eskimo Radiator."

He was the first to design and work out the mechanism for the evaporative cooler in the middle twenties. Oscar says he installed the first real evaporative cooler in his home at that time, at 1721 Lincoln in the early 1920's. This was the first one installed in a house in the valley of the sun that was functional.

Production of the evaporative cooler took place on a minor scale in the 1920's. Sears and Roebuck began to sell his coolers.

In 1934 excelsior pads largely replaced burlap and this was a monumental contribution. In the 1930's thousands were now being sold and other companies began to enter the field.

In 1939 two University of Arizona Professors conducted experiments to find the best designs for coolers, and circulated mimeographed instruction throughout the state entitled, "Cooling for the Arizona home."

By 1953 the booming business was approaching $40,000,000 annual sales. A score of companies were taking a piece of the pie. Sales later were over a million units a year produced in part by three Phoenix manufacturers: Palmer Manufacturing Company, Wright Manufacturing Company, and International Metal Products Company.

In 1952 the Palmer Manufacturing Company had six hundred employees. It was in the same year that Oscar sold his business. His coolers seem at least partly responsible for the rapidly growing wealth and population boom of many Western areas besides Arizona. They were to be sent to all parts of the world. Not only do they provide employment in cities like Phoenix, but as the world's first inexpensive air conditioning, they made homes and buildings habitable in hundreds of deserts, long before refrigeration cooling.

Oscar Palmer and his pioneers in this field, increased the productivity and financial gain of thousands of people. They made thousands of resorts and buildings tenable to northern tourists, many of whom settled or invested in Arizona.

This man who is associated with such brand names as "Snow-Breeze," "Sensible Coolers," "Frost-T-Aire," "Ice Berg," and "Eskimo," is indeed a great man. In the community in which he lived, he was noted for his philanthropy and total dedication to civic and charitable promotions. He tamed the searing summer and all Arizonans are cooler because of him. He died in 1985.

In the 1940's toward the end of the war, the air condition unit began to be sold. It was more costly to purchase and used more electricity. Companies like the Goettl Brothers, Carrier, Fedders, York and many others flooded the field.

Today with the energy crises, there is a big shift in the desert communities to evaporative coolers. Eventually, only the wealthy will be able to afford air conditioning with the rising costs of energy. The time is at hand for the rebirth of the evaporative cooler.

The golden epoch that gave rise to the birth of the evaporative cooler, has truly played a magnificent role in the history of Arizona. It is as important as the invention of gun powder, the steam engine, the auto, television, the rifle, and the computer.

Today Arizona is one of the leading states in the production and development of solar energy. Thousands of homes and buildings are being converted to this new advancement in heating and air cooling.

Today in the year 1992 heat and air conditioning bills are very expensive. The two companies that sell the said energies are Salt River Project and Arizona Public Service. They are the biggest utility companies in Arizona. Many people living in Arizona will tell you that they think that these companies ask too much for their products.

However, the fear of living in Arizona because of the heat of the summer is no longer a problem. Air conditioning makes life very pleasant in the summertime.

But the powerful sun in Arizona has taken its toll on Arizonans with the problem of skin cancer. Arizona leads the nation with sundry skin cancer cases because of the powerful rays of the sun. One must be careful at all times not to overdo sitting in the sun without the proper precautions for face and body exposure. While many come to Arizona to enjoy the sun for health reasons, research has shown that the overexposure to the sun can indeed be dangerous.

CHAPTER 20.
Famous People in Arizona History

"Take time to work, it is the price of success. Take time to think, it is the source of power. Take time to play, it is the secret of youth. Take time to read, it is the foundation of knowledge. Take time to worship, it is the highway of reverence. Take time for friendship, it is the source of happiness. Take time to love, it is the one sacrament of life."

Sue Jones
Historian

Arizona is noted for its famous and interesting men who have participated with their energies and talents to make it the great State that it is. Their number is legion. The author is attempting to name only a very few in this book. It would be impossible to name all of them.

Barry Morris Goldwater. If there was ever a politician who made an impact on his state and on the nation, it has to be Barry Goldwater. He is often called the father of the Republican party. A man of amazing political skills, the noted Senator from Arizona won the Republican nomination in 1964 for the presidency, but lost to Lyndon Johnson. Barry Goldwater was born in 1909 in Arizona, the son and grandson of pioneer merchants. Barry grew up in the rustic days of early Phoenix. As a young man he worked in his father's department store and took it over when he died. He was elected to the Phoenix city council. He later managed Howard Pyle's successful election to become the Republican governor of Arizona. His first Senate election was in 1952 when he defeated the popular incumbent, Ernest McFarland. As a senator he became the spokesman for his party and his state. When he retired in 1986 he was one of the most honored and celebrated senators in our nation's history. He is and was Mr. Republican.

The author interviewed the Senator in his home in 1994. He spoke about his long love affair with the state of Arizona and its people. He believes that Phoenix is well on its way to becoming one of the largest cities in the country. He favors gambling for the Indians in this state. But he opposes total gambling like they have in Nevada. He wants major league baseball to come to Arizona. He favors a dental school for Arizona but wonders why it was never given a big push by the legislature. He feels that we cannot build a second medical school at Arizona State University for we do not have the money. He does not favor a

136

major airport to be built between Phoenix and Tucson. The author was impressed with his keen mind at his age, his quick wit, his knowledge of the history of Arizona and his kind and warm hospitality. Like Marco Polo who told the world about the greatness of China so has Senator Goldwater told the world about the imperial majesty of Arizona.

Charles Trumbull Hayden. He was born in Windsor, Connecticut, on April 4, 1825, the son of James T. and Mary Hayden, both of whom were of distinguished colonial ancestry. An intelligent youth, he had the advantages of a good education and was teaching school in New Jersey by the time he was eighteen. Later he taught in Indiana and Missouri before the westward rolling wagons captured his interest.

In 1848 he entered the mercantile business, loading a wagon with goods and hauling it to Santa Fe where he marketed them. The following year he loaded fourteen wagons, hitched six yoke of oxen to each and again set out for Santa Fe, intending to set up in business, but a group of Californians, short of everything because of the gold rush of 1849, bought his whole outfit.

After another trip to Missouri, he moved to Santa Fe. In 1858, he moved his headquarters to Tucson, where he contracted with the government to furnish supplies to the soldiers in the region. He also did a brisk freight business with the mines, hauling supplies in and ore out.

Hayden's wagons often were attacked by Apaches, but he was, by this time, an experienced Indian fighter. One military report in 1863 noted that Hayden's train had been attacked by Apaches; but the Indians were driven off after eleven of them were killed, including one of their chiefs, Capinggan.

While in Tucson, Hayden was appointed the area's first probate judge, but according to a letter he wrote later in life, his duties were not too taxing.

"In the year I occupied the bench," he wrote, "there was no case of death, not a civil case, and only one criminal case before the court."

He added that five hundred Mexicans composed virtually the entire population of Tucson at that time and they settled their disputes in typical frontier fashion, without the aid of the courts.

Among his other traits was a keen desire to expand his business, and it was during a trip to Fort Whipple in 1870 for this purpose that he first saw the Salt River Valley. He found the river too high to ford and climbed a butte near present-day Tempe to get a better view. What he saw was a valley about fifteen miles wide through which flowed the Salt River for about forty miles westward to its junction with the Gila. Jack Swilling had completed the first irrigation ditch of modern times two years before, and already two thousand acres were under cultivation. Hayden was so impressed with what he saw that he returned to Tucson only long enough to collect his goods. Hastening back to the Salt River, he immediately built a store and established a ferry near where the Tempe Bridge is located today. The area became known as Hayden's Ferry.

In 1871, Swilling organized another irrigation company, the Tempe Irrigating Canal Company, and at his suggestion it offered two thousand inches of water, equivalent to seventeen shares in the company, to anyone who would construct a grist mill of approved capacity. Hayden accepted the offer and began construction in 1872. The mill went into operation in 1874, using water from an extension of the Kirkland-McKinney ditch to turn the grinding stones. The mill had a capacity of about two thousand pounds of flour a day.

No storage reservoirs, such as the Salt River Project has today, were in existence in the 1870's, so the farmers were somewhat at the mercy of the river. When it was high, there was enough water to fill all commitments, but when it was low, everyone took a cut, and Hayden was permitted to operate his mill only two days a week because agriculture had first priority on the water.

Although the man who became known as the Father of Tempe lost an 1874 bid for a seat in Congress, most ventures went well for him. Besides the store, the ferry and the mill, he owned the blacksmith shop, the carpenter shop and most of the rest of Hayden's Ferry, in addition to two stores in other locales and an interest in ranch property near Prescott. He helped organize several canal companies on the south side of the river, canals which eventually would become part of the Salt River Valley Water Users' Association system along with the Tempe Canal and other north side canals.

Perhaps, because he was too busy organizing canal companies and expanding his business enterprises, or perhaps because he never met the right girl, Hayden waited until 1876, when he was 51 years old to take a bride. In that year on October 4, he married Miss Sallie Calvert Davis in Nevada City, California, returning with her to Tempe in 1877. This well-educated, strong-willed pioneer apparently had found a perfect match, for his wife was described as a woman of "unusual force of character and strong intellectual endowments."

The Haydens had four children: Carl, who became and remained until 1968 one of the nation's most revered United States Senators; Sallie, who became a teacher; Mary, whose two sons continued to operate the flour mill; and Annie, who died in infancy.

In the year 1900, Charles Trumbull Hayden died, preceding his wife by seven years. He will be remembered as the man who always was willing to lend a helping hand, who commanded the respect and trust of all who knew him, and whose sincerity and integrity were never doubted. His monuments are the City of Tempe, which he founded; the life-giving canal system which he helped develop; and Arizona State University, which came into existence as Tempe Normal School, conceived in the mind of Charles Trumbull Hayden, who donated the land on which it was constructed.

Dwight Bancroft Heard. He was born in Boston on May 1, 1869. It was in Chicago in 1886 at the age of seventeen, he began his business career with a wholesale hardware firm. On August 10, 1894, he married Maie Clay Bartlett.

The following year the couple journeyed west to Arizona. While his father's enthusiasm for the untamed lands on the western horizon undoubtedly played a part in Heard's decision to move, of at least equal importance was a troublesome lung. Shortly after arriving in Arizona, he formed the Bartlett-Heard Land and Cattle Company in partnership with his father-in-law and two years later, established an investment and loan business.

The Bartlett-Heard firm purchased 7,500 acres of land south of the Salt River which were planted in grapes, oranges and grapefruit. Later it was subdivided into homesites, but Heard continued intensive farming of 1,100 acres which he planted with citrus, cotton, alfalfa, grain and grapes. With such extensive holdings, it is natural that irrigation was a dominant interest, and he was one of the staunchest advocates of federal legislation to permit the government to undertake reclamation projects. As one of the five persons named to the first Water Storage Commission of Maricopa County, he attempted to persuade Congress to pass the needed legislation. President McKinley seemed indifferent, however, and Congress stalled.

With the assassination of President McKinley on September 14, 1901, Theodore Roosevelt became President and the outlook appeared more favorable. Heard was a friend of Teddy Roosevelt, and he now used all his persuasive powers to urge the President to support an enlightened reclamation policy. His arguments and the arguments of others fell on receptive ears. In 1902, while Heard was in Washington, the National Reclamation Act was passed. The foundation was laid for development of the West.

Heard's friendship with the President was to bear further fruit, for Arizona was not the only area seeking an irrigation project. Heard argued, however, that the five conditions necessary for a successful irrigation project were present in Arizona: (1) an excellent watershed, (2) an easily dammable canyon, (3) tillable, fertile soil, (4) large reservoir capacity above the dam site, and (5) a climate providing a long growing season. There seems little doubt that Heard played a significant role in securing for Arizona the first project authorized under the National Reclamation Act.

Finding an acceptable method of repaying the government for construction of Roosevelt Dam proved difficult. Large landowners such as Heard resented proposals which would saddle them with a disproportionate share of the cost, while small landowners and holders of water rights were equally adamant that their portion of the cost be kept to a minimum. The need was plain, however, and despite heated controversy, a compromise plan was finally agreed upon. That decision made, some four thousand landowners formed the Salt River Valley Water Users' Association to finance construction of the dam. The association was incorporated on February 9, 1903.

Heard's achievements at this point in his life were considerable, but he was just getting started. He was to be a major figure in the fight to prevent joint statehood with New Mexico and in the organization of cooperative marketing associations for hay growers, cotton growers and grain growers.

In 1912 he followed his friend, President Roosevelt, into the Progressive movement and purchased The Arizona Republic, so the party would have a public organ in the territory. In 1924 he was the Republican candidate for Governor, but was defeated by about eight hundred votes by former Governor Hunt, 38,372 to 37,571.

In addition to furthering the development of an efficient irrigation system, one of Heard's prime concerns was the highway system, and he served as president of the Arizona Good Roads Association. A small sampling of his other affiliations could include the Conservation of Natural Resources Congress, the National Irrigation Congress, National Conservation Congress, Roosevelt Council of Boy Scouts of America, American National Livestock Association, U. S. Chamber of Commerce, Phoenix

Community Chest, World Cotton Conference and many others. He was an officer of virtually every organization with which he was associated.

Despite his many business interests, he took an active part in the life of his church, Trinity Episcopal Cathedral, and enjoyed fishing, golfing and playing tennis. He also found time to promote Arizona through magazine articles such as "Arizona's Irrigation Development," for The Earth.

During World War I he was chairman of the Arizona Council of Defense and with his knowledge of agriculture, succeeded in greatly increasing the state's agricultural production. He also was chairman for the War Camp Community Service and in recognition of these activities was appointed a captain in the Officers Reserve Corps, Eight Corps Area.

Both Heard and his wife were greatly interested in prehistoric research, and they left to the people of Arizona a prehistoric community house which they had uncoverd two miles east of Phoenix and a museum to house their collection of the art and handicraft of primitive peoples. Both Pueblo Grande and Heard Museum are major assets of modern-day Phoenix.

Dwight Bancroft Heard died on March 14, 1929. He was survived by Mrs. Heard, who lived until 1951, and by their son, Bartlett Bradford Heard, who had been born on December 17, 1898. Bartlett Heard and his family reside in California.

The Arizona Legislature memorialized him after his death, and a Phoenix Gazette editorial called him "fearless, positive and forceful — the very essence of constructive action."

Perhaps the most fitting tribute to this man who had a major role in formation of the Salt River Valley Water Users Association and construction of Roosevelt Dam was by historian John R. Murdock, who wrote:

"In sober truth, Dwight B. Heard ought to be listed among the half dozen great Americans who are responsible for the extensive achievement of conservation and reclamation throughout the West . . ."

Wilson Wesley Dobson. Dobson arrived in the Salt River Valley in 1886 from California and was impressed with what he saw. He knew fertile land when he saw it and crouched down in the hostile desert to touch the soil and let it run through his fingers. He decided he would homestead this quarter section of land, just outside of the small community of Mesa, Arizona.

One of the first things he did was to build himself a shelter which was more of a shack than anything else. Its size was approximately six feet by ten feet. The floor was dirt.

For three years he would live there under the crudest conditions. Days he would spend working for his neighbors, either irrigating their fields or chopping wood. In the evening he worked his own land, clearing away the mesquite and palo verdes and cacti. His neighbors said they could hear his axe late into the night.

But when those three years passed, Dobson had something to show for his labors. His farm was a going concern, so much so that eventually he was able to acquire adjoining properties, bringing his total acreage to 640.

After building a new house, using rocks which he hauled from the Salt River bed as the foundation, he returned to Canada to marry his sweetheart, Emma Argue, and bring her to his adopted country. She would bear him three children, Wilson, Harold, and a girl, Hazel, who died tragically at a young age. After his wife died, he remarried.

As a farmer, he of course realized the value of irrigation and canal systems, and it was no wonder that he became active in the affairs of the Utah Canal Company, eventually becoming a director, then president, of that concern.

Dobson was one of the farmers who actually helped in the construction of the Utah Extension and Eureka Canal. In the future, his experiences with the Utah Canal Company would serve him in good stead.

W. W. Dobson was also a member of the Fourth Legislature, serving during the years 1919-1920. But it was a position he did not like very much. He was disdainful of backslapping and horse-trading, and did not hold the label "politician" in high regard.

He was a fine, honorable man, and a steady contributor to the Methodist Church, which he helped to establish. He was a member of the church board and school board.

His feats of stamina and endurance are legion. The quarter section he initially cleared was done solely by pick, shovel and axe. He was an expert axeman, and made every lick count. The story is told that he once had a contract job of cutting wood, for which he was paid by the cord. When his employer came by to see how he was doing, W. W. explained that he wasn't feeling well and hadn't done very much. The man was amazed to find a woodpile half as high as a house.

There was the time that Dr. Moeur of Tempe told W. W. to rest and relax, that he shouldn't drive himself so hard. The prescription was a trip to the mountains. W. W. went willingly enough, but he stayed only half as long as the good doctor recommended, and while there, cut two carloads of cedar posts!

In summer, when the growing season was over in the Valley, he'd go up to his farms in Canada, and supervise the wheat harvest.

He loved to plant things and watch them grow. The canal bank near his house was covered with fig trees. Many a time he would join the rest of his family and relatives in harvesting the figs and peeling and making them ready for preserving. He had hundreds of these trees, and welcomed travelers and picnickers from Phoenix and the surrounding area to pick them.

W. W. had a sweet tooth for honey. Often he would go off with mask and gloves, come back several hours later, and pass out the sweet stuff to whoever was present at his home.

Dobson was active to the end, but unfortunately, as he grew older, he had many sleepless nights. He also had trouble reaching for a word, and this perplexed this vital, dynamic man.

While visiting in Canada with his wife, he attempted to fix the leaking roof of a house he was renting. On the roof, he suffered a stroke which caused him to lose his eyesight. Even that didn't stop him. In his later years, when he had moved to town, he would spend time visiting his sister who lived on Main Street in Mesa, walking there unaided.

Wilson Wesley Dobson died on May 19, 1940. He was one of the last of that rugged breed who wanted something better and would get it by the sweat of his brow.

John P. Orme. "It is given to but few men to render conspicuous and useful service in nation, state and community for 60 years."

That eulogy was given to John P. Orme in an obituary notice November 13, 1936. It was a tribute to a man whose death commanded notice with headlines reading: "Empire Builder of Valley Dies;" and "Community Builder Helped Develop Valley Area."

Another name was given to him, too, "Uncle John." That's how he was known to his pioneer friends. Instead of "Uncle John" however, it well could have been "Uncle Arizona," since he helped lay the groundwork for Arizona's present water supply and prosperity.

143

John P. Orme, an Easterner, came to Arizona for his health and entered upon a new career here — the story of many modern Arizonans. Sandwiched in between the words of the above sentence was a multi-faceted service to the Valley that lives on today.

A heritage of government service accompanied John Pickney Orme when he entered this world on November 28, 1852, at Montgomery County, Maryland. The son of Charles and Deborah (Pleasants) Orme, he was a direct descendant of Governor Pleasants of Virginia.

Apparently, however, Orme had no early intentions of becoming a statesman. In 1866 he entered Missouri State University at Columbia, studied civil engineering, and was graduated in 1868. As a resident engineer for the Texas and Pacific Railroad in Southeastern Texas, he helped construct one of the first railways between Missouri and Texas.

However, the Lone Star State was not to be his home. Orme wandered across much of the West before settling in Arizona. While serving as a civil engineer in Texas and Louisiana he had become a victim of malaria. His attacks of chills and fever sent him in quest of a healthier climate and he left Texas for Colorado. He stayed there briefly before journeying to Los Angeles to work on a pier. This, however, only aggravated his malaria condition and he came to Arizona.

Phoenix, and the forbidding desert country of rocks, mountains, and sparse vegetation with hot days and cool nights might have seemed an unhealthy country for a frail, bespectacled man whose five-foot, seven-inch frame was racked often with attacks of malaria. Nonetheless, Orme thrived here.

His early employment in Arizona, when Phoenix had a population of only one thousand, was as a mule skinner in the Yuma area. For a short time he freighted wheat to Flagstaff, but a shower of Indian arrows on one of his trips convinced him there were safer ways of making a livelihood. He opened a corral in Maricopa, bought forty acres near the present Phoenix Country Club site, and soon thereafter obtained eight hundred acres of land in the Cartwright area and became a cattle rancher.

The need of water for his livestock and crops led him to a study of irrigation, and he rapidly became an authority on the subject. His engineering background stood him in good stead when, with his two brothers, Henry and Lin, he built the eighteen mile long Arizona Canal. John also served as superintendent and director of the canal.

Marriage accompanied Orme's early ranching and farming endeavors. He met his wife, Ella Tompkins, in Phoenix where she had been living since leaving Texas at the age of eight. They were married March 8, 1879.

To this union were born four children — Charles Henry, later to have a "Senior" attached to his name; Ora D.; Winifred D., and Clara E. A strong family man, Orme often told his children, "There is no success in the world if your family's not reared properly." Tragedy struck the family with Mrs. Orme's death in 1898, and her loss deeply affected Orme. He turned to a cousin, Kate Lackland, for aid in rearing the children, and he remained single the rest of his life.

Orme apparently filled this void in his life by turning to public service, for the period shortly after his wife's death found him extremely active in community affairs. Having no hobbies, he plunged himself into his work and politics. "His hobby was work; he was a slave driver; he never stayed still himself and he never let anybody else stay still," recalls his son, Charles Henry, "It seemed like he always was on a school board."

The Arizona pioneer became a member of the Salt River Valley Water Users' Association board of governors in 1904 and continued in that capacity until 1909. The following year he became the Association's second president, succeeding B. A. Fowler, and served until May, 1918.

An active Democrat, he was on the Maricopa County board of supervisors for nine years, four of which were as board chairman. He also was a member of the Arizona Constitutional Convention in 1911. Historians refer to him as being known for his well-defined plans, an apparent carry-over of his engineering talents to the political field.

A gregarious man, Orme also became active in numerous organizations. He was a member of the Ancient Order of United Workmen and Independent Order of Odd Fellows, both in Phoenix. His Masonic affiliations included Blue Lodge, Chapter, Commandery and Shrine.

Orme did much to direct Arizona's growth in unheralded capacities. "He was a very persuasive man who worked behind the scenes," points out his son, Charles Henry, "It was he and Joe Kibbey who got warring factions together" in the water disputes of the era.

Despite his intense interest in the serious problems of early Arizona, Orme was a man with a sense of humor. "He was a great joker," recalls Charles Henry Orme. "At the dedication of Theodore Roosevelt Dam in 1911, he and Teddy Roosevelt and Bishop Atwood, a prominent Episcopalian at that time, stayed overnight together in the same room. My father delighted in telling how Bishop Atwood wouldn't let him and Teddy go to bed until they said their prayers, "You two old sinners won't get any sleep until you say those prayers," the Bishop told them.

Orme's interest in politics just came naturally to him. He was politically oriented and at the age of 71, he stepped into the role of an Arizona lawmaker. Making his legislative debut in 1923, Orme twice was elected to the House of Representatives. His son was to carry on the tradition becoming an Arizona state senator in 1952 and serving four terms. The son, Charles, was just as respected in legislative circles as his Dad was.

Another family interest, concern with good education, rubbed off on Charles. In 1929 he became the founder of the Orme School, 75 miles north of Phoenix. Orme school enjoys the reputation of being one of the best private schools in the country.

John P. Orme made his name known throughout Arizona as an engineer, rancher, reclamationist, statesman and educator. He died on November 12, 1936.

Louis Clarence Hill was the designer and supervisory engineer of the construction of Theodore Roosevelt Dam, Arizona's great water storage facility. This accomplishment alone launched him upon a long, brilliant career in the construction of many more large, successful dams in the West, including the great Hoover Dam.

In the years that followed, Hill never forgot the importance of the Theodore Roosevelt Dam nor his long personal and often frustrating involvement in this massive creation. Before he died on November 6, 1938, at his home in Pasadena, California, he expressed the wish that his ashes be entombed in Theodore Roosevelt Dam. Accordingly, a receptacle containing his ashes was placed in the top of the dam directly below a bronze marker at the south end of the structure. Hill died at age seventy-three.

146

Son of a jewelry merchant, Hill attended schools in Detroit. Later, he studied at the University of Michigan, where he earned a degree in civil engineering in 1886, and a second degree in electrical engineering four years later.

His early jobs were varied. He began as draftsman for Detroit Pipe & Foundry. This led to work as a leveler and transitman with the Duluth, Redwing & Southern Railway, and to a position of resident engineer for the Great Northern Railroad. Finally he accepted professorships in physics and electrical engineering at the Colorado School of Mines.

A sense of restlessness continued to plague him, a nagging feeling that life held a deeper purpose for him. It brought him to welcome his appointment on June 8, 1903, as an engineer in the U. S. Reclamation Service.

Two months later he came face to face with his purpose in life, although he did not recognize it at the time. He was assigned to the Salt River Valley in central Arizona.

Hill was placed in charge of the Roosevelt project in the spring of 1904. He remained in this position until March, 1911.

Roosevelt Dam was an engineering challenge from the very first. Yet the initial stone of the huge structure was not set down until September 20, 1906, and the last stone laid on February 6, 1911.

Much of the preliminary work was devoted to the building of access roads, using Indian labor from the White Mountain Apache tribes. Hill lauded the ability of these Apaches as dependable unskilled laborers and often sent them out on the job in unsupervised squads.

It was necessary to erect a cement plant due to the remoteness of the job site. Hill built such a plant. He also built a small lumber mill and provided needed power by constructing a thirteen-mile power canal for generating electricity.

Each step forward was a tribute to Hill and the men who worked for him, for they had no previous projects of this kind to guide their operations. Decisions were made quickly and with conviction. Hill and his men were motivated by one mutual desire, to build Roosevelt Dam and make it a worthy prototype for similar future projects.

In 1911, the 284-foot high structure, from bedrock, was completed with its turbines ready to generate electricity. Roosevelt was the largest dam built to that date in the country, but the cost had reached the frightening amount of $5.4 million.

Senator Harold Giss. Extravagant claims are made often in the world of politics but no one will deny that the number one man in the history of modern Yuma, was Harold C. Giss. This elder statesman and civic leader supreme, dominated the political and civic life of Yuma and Arizona from 1948 until he died in 1973. During that time he was one of the most influential men in legislative circles in this State.

He was born in Minneapolis, Minnesota, on February 5, 1906. When Harold was ten years old, the family left for Los Angeles.

He married Goldie Stool of Del Rio, Texas, and they first arrived in Yuma, in 1938. He purchased a department store, the Emporium, and he was its guiding light for many years.

Senator Giss was blessed with three fine sons, Maurice, Kenneth and Gerald. Maurice was the Executive Director of the Bicentennial Commission for the State of Arizona in 1976.

He entered politics in 1948, when he was first elected to the House of Representatives. In two years, he was elected Senator and served with distinction in that capacity until he died.

The esteem in which Senator Giss was held in Yuma, was vividly manifested on May 15, 1965. On that day one thousand state, city and county leaders (including your author) gathered to pay homage to him at a testimonial dinner. The author was greatly impressed by the respect and love displayed by all for this great man.

He was a man who cared for people. Many will testify that he was the best lawmaker in the history of the State of Arizona. He left his mark on Arizona as few have done. People loved Senator Giss.

General George Crook (1828-1890). He was recognized by all as an able and talented military leader. General William T. Sherman thought that General Crook was the greatest Indian fighter in the West and the best the army ever had. He grew up on a farm in Ohio and was a graduate of West Point, finishing in the bottom half of his class. After serving in Ohio and on the west coast, he was sent to Arizona by President Ulysses S. Grant. He was placed in command of the Department of Arizona in 1871. His number one enemy was the Apaches. By 1873 he was famous for using Indian scouts and fought the Indians only when he had to and relative peace reigned in the Arizona territories. The Indians were on reservations but it was a peace that

148

was eventually broken. He never did conquer the Apaches but was a compassionate man who made sure that his command did not use excess in punishing the Indians. Although Chief Red Cloud had fought against him, he was friendly to the General. Upon the death of the General, Chief Red Cloud said: "He never lied to us. His words gave the people hope." Many called him the "terrible and the just". He never used profanity which made him something special among his troops.

General Crook left the Gila country in 1886. After years of Indian fighting, he defined his position by saying:

> "It should not be expected that an Indian who has lived as a barbarian all his life will become an angel the moment he comes on a reservation and promises to behave himself. Or that he has that strict sense of honor that a person should have who has had the advantage of civilization all his life, and the benefit of a moral training and character which has been transmitted to him through a long line of ancestors. It requires constant watching and knowledge of their character to keep them from going wrong. They are children in ignorance not in innocence. I do not wish to be understood as in the least palliating their crimes, but I wish to say a word to stem the torrent of invective and abuse which has and had been indulged in against the whole Apache race.

> I have no knowledge of a case on record where a white man has been convicted and punished for defrauding an Indian. Greed and avarice on the part of the whites...... in other words the almighty dollar is at the bottom of nine tenths of all our Indian trouble."

The Gila, River of the Southwest by Edwin Corle, Page 305

CHAPTER 21.

The Black Man in Arizona

"There comes a time when the cup of endurance runs over, and men are no longer willing to be plunged into an abyss of injustice where they experience the bleakness of corroding despair. I hope, sirs, you can understand our legitimate and unavoidable impatience."

Martin Luther King, Jr.

If one is to write a history of Arizona, some mention should be made of the great contributions of the black man. Very few books on Arizona history have made any real reference to these great people. We shall attempt to peruse some of their significant contributions.

The first black man mentioned in Arizona history has to be the black slave, Estevan or Estevanico. By religion he was a Moslem. He departed Culican, Mexico, on March 7, 1539, with the famous Father Marcos De Niza, a Franciscan missionary. They are famous in history for their expedition to find the famed, seven, gold cities of Cibola.

Many of the forty niners going to California in the big gold strike of 1849, were black men. Many believed that they had a sixth sense for finding gold and they were welcomed by most white men.

Arizona had many Black cowboys. Between 1870 and 1900, Black cowboys made a big impact on our history but few history books–record this information. Black ranch hands constituted nearly one fourth of the work force of the West.

John Swain died in Tombstone, Arizona, in 1945, at the age of ninety-nine. He was a famous black cowboy. Employed by John Slaughter for many years, Swain gained a reputation as the right hand man for Slaughter as he built his cattle empires in New Mexico and Texas. He is buried in Tombstone, Arizona, in the famous Boothill Cemetery.

The Blacks played a big role in the military history of Arizona and for that matter, throughout the West. The Blacks were known as Buffalo soldiers, so nicknamed by the Indians in respect to the sacred animal. Also the Blacks had wooly hair and it was likened to the Buffalo mane.

The Blacks served with distinction in the West. Altogether, they comprised about fifteen percent of the military in the West in the approximately fifty years after the Civil War.

The author had the privilege of talking with Sergeant John Campbell in his home in Phoenix. He is the last Buffalo soldier alive who served at Fort Huachuca, arriving there in 1912. He pointed out that the Indians in our history were very fond of the Black soldier. Fort Huachuca was a good duty post and the summers were not too hot because of the higher elevation in that area. He is proud of the thirty-three years he served in the Army and states he was treated very well by the command structure.

The Blacks fought usually in all Black outfits. Officially both the 9th and 10th U. S. Cavalry were created out of a Federal Act of July, 1866. It determined that to the regiments of Cavalry now in service, shall be added four regiments, two of which shall be composed of colored men. At Jefferson Barracks in Missouri, Lt. Col. Benjamin Grierson, a former music teacher, who was a former war hero for the North, was the first commander of the 10th Cavalry. In New Orleans the 9th Cavalry was organized by Colonel Edward Hatch.

Among the commissioned officers of the 10th Cavalry in their glorious history, was Lieutenant John J. Pershing, who later was to lead the U. S. Army in World War I. Also, Colonel Leonard Wood, served with these fine soldiers. He was to become eventually the Chief of Staff during World War I. Only two black officers were to serve these units in Arizona covering a period of some fifty years. They were Henry O. Flipper and Charles Young, both graduates of West Point Military Academy.

During the 1920's and 1930's Blacks migrated to new settlements around the State. Blacks around Tucson attempted a mining venture in 1912, led by a certain J. W. Miller. It was to prove to be unsuccessful.

A memorable event in the history of Phoenix was the celebrated visit by Booker T. Washington. He was guest speaker at the Emancipation Proclamation celebration, commemorated on October 23 and 24, 1911.

The school system for years in Arizona had separate schools for the Whites and the Blacks. Tucson's first Jim Crow School was opened when the city had 14 Black families. The first classes were in a small house at Sixth Street and Sixth Avenue. Phoenix Union Colored High School was organized in 1922. In 1926 the school moved into an adequate building at 415 East Grant that was to house it until 1953.

The Klu Klux Klan paraded in Phoenix in the 1920's and was very active. It often visited White and Black churches. While visiting the Blacks, they would put money in the collection plate. They left the message loud and clear that they would support the Black community, as long "as they remained in their place." The stigma of discrimination was accelerated more after Arizona became a State. In territorial days, the Blacks were more accepted in the White community. Statehood brought in more Southerners with deeper dislike for the Blacks.

The author visited the separate black grade school in Nogales, Arizona in 1950. He was warmly received many times by the genial and competent, black faculty. But it was apparent that in Nogales as well as in other parts of the State, the Blacks did not have equal buildings or grounds in comparison to their White brethren. Carver High School in Phoenix for a long time felt this burden.

Phoenix Union High School District took action on desegregation a year prior to the United States Supreme Court decision of 1954.

Two black families who came to Phoenix around the turn of the century were the Crumps and the Rossers. Both families settled in the predominantly black East Jefferson Street. Both families still live in Phoenix.

Miss Irene Rosser lived on East Jefferson and was the surviving daughter of Mr. and Mrs. Richard Rosser who migrated from Georgia with a large family. Miss Rosser who in a personal chat, gave the author the interesting experience of interviewing her and discussing the early days in Phoenix, at her home. She remembered early Phoenix well. Just about everyone slept outside in the summertime. There was the iceman who brought the ice each day to the homes. The food was more nutritious than it is today. And people had more fun in the 1900's than they do today. Hay rides and barbecues were the big events. There was running water in the homes and the Blacks were very few. Miss Rosser did not mind the heat without air conditioning but the dust storms were absolutely ferocious.

The National Association for the Advancement of Colored People came into Phoenix in the 1940's. The Urban League founded a branch office in Phoenix in 1945.

During the 1960's when the rest of the nation was pushing civil rights and there was civil rebellion in the land, Arizona assumed its maturity and passed a Public Accommodation ordinance as well as a civil rights package.

All in all, Blacks have made their mark in the history of Arizona. They number about 95,000 in the state today. To say that there is no discrimination in Arizona today is not true.

In the general election of 1990, Arizona failed to pass legislation to enact a paid holiday to honor Martin Luther King, Jr. Since it is one of the few states in the nation that does not have such a day, Arizona quickly received the reputation on a national scale that Arizona was racist. The so called reputation is not true, for Arizona is not a racist state. Like all states we have people who have extremist views against civil rights and we have many who favor civil rights.

Arizona will again vote in the general election of 1992 on the issue. The vote is expected to be for a paid Martin Luther King holiday for state employees. As it is now, we do honor Martin Luther King, Jr. with a holiday but it is not a paid holiday for the state workers. Arizona is known as a convention center for many groups from all over the nation. Many have refused to come here since we do not have a paid holiday to honor this man. It has cost the state millions of dollars in lost revenue.

CHAPTER 22.

Arizona Territorial Prison In Yuma

In 1873, the U.S. Army was maintaining 13 major posts and six campsites in Arizona. This was the year that the Apache wars were ended temporarily by the famous truce between Indian Agent Jonathan Jeffords and Indian Chief Cochise.

Ray Brandes
Historian

The Arizona Territorial Prison is located in Yuma, Arizona. It was in operation for thirty-three years, 1876-1909, and renamed the "Hell Hole" by earlier inmates. It had some of the roughest and toughest characters the West has ever known. Some writers describe it as a Desert Alcatraz.

Arizona had so many criminals during the 70's and 80's that the town jails could not secure all the prisoners without a few escaping. Officers of the law were effective and many arrests and convictions were evident. For this reason, a prison was needed badly in Arizona. During the year 1875, the prison was authorized by the legislature. The cost of the prison was to be $25,000, but the small sum was used up before the completion of the prison. The final completion of the prison was accomplished by the inmates.

Location of the Territorial Prison at Yuma was a legislative feat of the 1875 session, in which Jose Redondo played a leading part. That he came to be known as the "father of the penitentiary" was, however, doubtless due not so much to the part he played in the legislation, as to the fact that the famous institution was built under his direction. The competition of numerous towns, principally Prescott, Florence, and Phoenix to secure the prison had apparently been settled by the legislature of 1873, through the passage of a bill naming Phoenix as the site. But no funds for construction were provided, as it was expected then that the cost would be met by the Federal Government. Thereby Phoenix lost its opportunity to become a penal colony instead of the capital city. The Yuma strategists under the leadership of Councilman Redondo and Representative R. B. Kelly, had the bill amended to read "Yuma." When the measure passed, Redondo was himself chosen by joint vote of the two houses as a member of the Board of Prison Commissioners. The other members were David Neahr of Yuma and Wm. H. Hardy of Mohave County.

The act establishing the prison at Yuma provided for a bond issue of $25,000, bearing ten percent interest and payable in five years. In November, 1875, the Commission sold the bonds to A. Luther, of San Francisco, the only bidder, for $21,265.62. With these funds a plant was constructed consisting of adobe walls five and a half feet thick at the base, and three feet at the first floor, built on a solid rock foundation; two stone cells, and an adobe building containing two prison rooms estimated to a capacity of thirty prisoners, a kitchen, dining room, hallroom for guards, superintendent's quarters, a water reservoir, boiler and engine and a well equipped blacksmith shop.

In his message to the 1877 Legislature, Governor Safford acknowledged that the Commissioners had performed their duties faithfully and well. "The whole work," he says, "seems to have been done in the most substantial manner and the prison is considered by those who have examined it, as secure a place for the confinement of prisoners as can be found in most of the older states." He was also pleased to be able to state, "that the money appropriated for the construction of the prison had been expended in an economical manner, and considered that the thanks of the people are due to the Commissioners for their services, which they have given without pecuniary reward."

The Arizona Territorial Penitentiary was a model for cleanliness. Most of the prisoners took some pride in keeping it that way. This fact, no doubt, tended to raise the morals of the convicts.

Well-cooked, wholesome meals were prepared in the prison kitchen and served in the immaculately clean dining room. The prisoners worked rather hard all day and they were kept better satisfied with good food. Instead of the policy enforced in prisons today, not allowing prisoners to talk at meal time, the prisoners in the Yuma prison chatted, visited, and enjoyed themselves the same as any other large group at mealtime.

The occupations of the prisoners were interesting. Of five hundred admitted during a certain period, three hundred were laborers or Indians. The latter was listed as having no occupation. There were twenty carpenters, four miners and four bartenders. Other vocations represented were a jeweler, author, bootblack, lady vaquero, jockey and politician.

The prison buildings are squat. They have decayed quite a bit since its closing. The prison looks like a medieval fortress. On all corners of the prison walls were guard towers, manned by rifle men who commanded every foot of the enclosed prison walls. The inside of the prison consisted of the main cell blocks, prisoners mess hall, exercise yard, blacksmith shop, bull pen, recreation hall for Sundays, woman's ward, and tuberculosis ward.

On the north side of the prison is the "sally port". There also is the mess hall, the stables, the arsenal, superintendent's cottage and the main guard tower.

Every one of the cells is stunted. The cells are nine feet by eight with a high domed ceiling. Inside the cells are two tiers of bunks. There is no wash bowl or any type of furniture. There are no toilet facilities, except a galvanized bucket which was emptied but once a day.

In the months of May through September the heat comes to Yuma. Sometimes the temperatures would soar as high as 120 degrees in the shade. The town people at night slept on the porches with dampened sheets to get some measure of comfort.

In 1885 an electric power plant was installed in the prison, and from then on the main cell house was ventilated by an electric blower.

In reading most of the prison physician's reports, sickness did not prevail at the prison. Only 79 prisoners died from disease, 2.6% of the total prisoners incarcerated. Of that number only six died from pneumonia.

If the prisoners disobeyed while in prison, they were sent to a place called the dungeon or "snake den." The prisoners were sent there and lived on bread and water. The cell was blasted out of solid rock. You entered the cell by a narrow passageway. The cell was about ten by ten in complete darkness, except when the sun was directly overhead. There was hardly any ventilation. This was a place to test a man's soul. The prisoner had no bed except bare ground to sleep on. He was kept shackled. There were not even blankets or a mattress for some comfort. There was no contact with the outside world except for his daily ration.

156

There is no record of any "Crazy Hole" at the prison. Insane inmates were sent to the Asylum in Stockton, California, until 1885 and after that to Phoenix, where the Territorial Asylum was established.

Efforts were made by the superintendents to keep the prisoner occupied without relaxing any of the strict discipline. Many of the men on good behavior were employed with various jobs. Some in the blacksmith shop, around the stables, in the mattress factory, tailor shop, mess hall, and in various other jobs. Trustees of the prison were relieved of some of the hard work.

The men who were hard core convicts had it really tough. They probably wished they had died a thousand times before they were through with their sentence. These criminals were the real troublemakers, incorrigibles, hardcore men. They had to break rocks all day. It was a continuing process. They also made adobes which were not only used for new prison construction, but were sold to the township for their own use. This type labor for prisoners meant long hours in the almost unbearable summer heat.

One of the most interesting sites upon entering the Yuma Territorial Prison is the main guard tower. It is located just outside the west prison wall. The structure is high, with open sides and a sloping roof. It would remind you of a bandstand in the earlier era when on Sunday afternoon, concerts were the order of the day. In time of a jail break, the noise of rifle bullets from its catwalks, was certainly no type of music to the ears of the desperate men trying to escape.

The science of penology, practiced Arizona style, circa 1875, was not very advanced. If you had tuberculosis, you were put in a separate TB cell. If you were insane, you were put in an insane cell. If you misbehaved, you were put in the "dungeon." And if you died, you were buried in the prison cemetery, where may be seen today the graves of 104 unfortunate beings.

Among those present at Yuma was Buckskin Frank Leslie, scout, marksman and Indian fighter and all-around Tombstone character. Once at a theatre in Tombstone, watching a performance from the orchestra, Buckskin Frank became angry at a drunken cowboy sprawled in an upper box with his feet on the rail. In the middle of the show he drew his six-gun and shot the heel off the cowboy's boot, which persuaded the cowboy thereafter to keep his feet where they belonged. It was not for this

157

though, that Buckskin Frank was sent to Yuma but for plugging a damsel called Molly Bradshaw. He received, for that feat of marksmanship, a life term in prison.

Throughout the history of the prison there were about 29 women inmates. Among those present was Pearl Hart. Pearl Hart was not convicted of holding up a stage coach, but she did participate in a stage coach hold-up outside of Globe. She was arrested around Bisbee. So far as anybody knows, that was the only crime Pearl ever committed, but she made an awfully good thing of it. She was written up in a New York newspaper and a national magazine and eventually went into vaudeville. There she exploited audiences with hairy and largely fictitious accounts of her escapades in the terrible Yuma prison.

Surely the toughest of them all, though, was Elana Estrada, a Latin spitfire with what impressionable journalists of the period were pleased to describe as "Cat's eyes." But it wasn't her eyes that made Elana famous. It was her passion for thoroughness. She was in the Yuma prison, or so we're told, for having killed her man and then, for good measure, cutting out his heart and slapping him in the face with it.

The story of the prison is complicated since the rules changed with each superintendent. One write-up, by a visitor, tells of the prisoners entering the mess hall unchained and conversing as "travelers at a wayside inn."

Another write-up gives a different picture. The prisoners were chained in groups of five or six, and no conversations were allowed at any time in the mess hall.

Of course, the cruel and sadistic angle is always played up by writers and much of the good treatment is ignored. It is possible and probably true that some individual guards were cruel; but then, this condition exists in many penal institutions today.

Other stories vary too — there are four published versions of the riot in which Mrs. Charles Ingalls, wife of the Superintendent, played a part. All vary, some with great stretch of the imagination. Other stories are written with an eye to giving the public an exciting story — factual or not.

The following is a complete and accurate list of the superintendents of the Territorial Prison at Yuma. The last prisoners were moved to Florence in September, 1909. A letter from Thomas Rynning shows that 180 short-term prisoners and 18 long-term prisoners were moved to Florence at that time.

1875—William A. Werninger
1876—Geo. M. Thurlow
1881—C. V. Meeden
1883—F. S. Ingalls
1886—Thomas Gates
1888—John H. Behan
1890—F. S. Ingalls
1891—M. M. McInernay
1893—Wm. K. Meade
1893—Thomas Gates
1896—Mike J. Nugent
1897—John W. Dorrington
1898—Herbert Brown
1902—William M. Griffith
1904—R. F. Daniels
1905—Jerry Millay
1907—Thomas Rynning

The monthly salary of a Superintendent was about $250.00 plus his residence and food for his table. All transportation was furnished. Prison manpower was furnished for yard work and house work. The wage of the assistant superintendent was about half of the Superintendent's salary. The Guards were paid from seventy-five to one-hundred dollars per month. This was good pay considering the value of the dollar in those days and there were no deductions as one has today.

After the close of the Prison in 1909, it was the location for classes for Yuma High School. They were held at the Prison until proper facilities could be built. Because of this temporary shelter for the student body, Criminals became the nickname of the school to this day.

One of the last Prison Doctors was Dr. R. R. Knotts. He was never appointed Prison Physician. He was an assistant to Dr. Clymer, an appointed Prison Physician, and did perform the final examinations on the last convicts to be transferred to Florence. He lived in retirement in Yuma and the author spent many hours talking to him about the Prison. Dr. Knotts told me that the Prison was not as bad as some described it in sundry writings and from legends that were growing from nowhere. He pointed out to me that it was not a sadistic place. It was rather an average institution following standard rules and procedures for a penal colony of its time. There was understanding and even friendship among the guards and convicts. Towards the last years of its existence, a Prison band was formed with about forty members. The band played only within the walls and it was extremely popular. Concerts were held only on

Sunday afternoons and they never seemed long enough for the prisoners. Also a church choir composed of young ladies from the various churches in Yuma, came to sing. Dr. Knotts made it clear that many of the harsh stories about the prison related to its early years. As he saw it, it was one of the best institutions in the West.

The historical prison also has a fascinating museum which is open to the public. Clarissa Brown Winsor who died in 1974, was a Yuma civic leader who founded the museum and was its first curator. In 1986 she was inducted in the Arizona Women's Hall of Fame. She joins 33 other outstanding women in the long history of Arizona who have received this honor.

Historical items in the museum include Pearl Hart's gun, camel bones, dice found in the ruins of Gila city, a dinner plate used by the famous Dick Wick Hall of Salome, Arizona, a sword carried by Hi Jolly, Arizona's most celebrated Camel Driver, ostrich eggs and feathers from one of the Arizona ranches (ostrich feathers was a big business in Arizona in its early history), gold mining equipment, postage stamp collections, old currency along with coins and sundry other items of great historical interest.

CHAPTER 23.

ARIZONA Kaleidoscope

"I even heard the complaint made that the thermometer failed to show the true heat because the mercury dried up. Everything dries; wagons, men dry; chickens dry, there is no juice left in anything, living or dead, by the close of the summer in Yuma. Chickens hatched at this season, as old fort Yumers say, come out of the shell ready cooked."

J. Ross Browne, in Adventures
in Apache Country, 1864

SPANISH PERIOD — 1528-1821

1528-36	Odyssey of Cabeza de Vaca stimulates desire to explore northern frontier of Mexico.
1539	Fray Marcos de Niza plods northward from Mexico.
1540-42	Francisco Vasquez de Coronado leads grand expedition to Arizona, New Mexico, and Kansas; white men first see Grand Canyon.
1582-83	Antonio de Espejo leads mining exploration up Rio Grande into New Mexico, then westward into Arizona.
1589-1607	Juan de Onate's party explores northern Arizona to Gulf of California.
1600	Franciscan missionaries attempting conversion of Indians in New Mexico and northeastern Arizona.
1608	City of Santa Fe founded by Pedro de Peralta.
1680	Pueblo revolt strikes Spanish culture on northern frontier.
1687-1711	Father Eusebio Francisco Kino brings Christianity to Indians of Pimeria Alta.
1696	Mission of Tumacacori established.
1700	Father Kino lays foundation of first Mission of San Xavier del Bac.
1736	Miraculous silver discovery (planchas de plata) at Arizona.

1751	Pimeria uprising against Spanish officials and priests.
1752	Presidio at Tubac established to subdue Indian revolt.
1767	King Carlos III expels Jesuits from Spanish realm.
1768	Father Francisco Garces takes charge at San Xavier as Franciscans are assigned to Arizona.
1774	Garces accompanies Anza on expedition to find route from Sonora to the western sea.
1775-76	Second Anza-Garces expedition; Garces travels widely in Arizona.
1776	Presidio garrison moved from Tubac to Tucson; Spain adopts new plan for controlling northern frontier.
1781	Yuma Massacre blights Spanish settlement in Arizona; Garces martyred.
1785-1810	Apaches pacified by bribes; prosperity in Pimeria Alta.
1810-1821	Northern provinces neglected as Spanish colonies in New World revolt.

MEXICAN PERIOD — 1821-1848

1821	Santa Fe trade route opened.
1823	First Texas settlements by Americans. Wagons of the Santa Fe trade reach Arizona.
1824-1840	American mountain men trap along Arizona streams for beaver and find traces of placer gold.
1830's	Scalp hunters roam Southwest to earn bounty payments offered in Mexico for Apache scalps.
1846	Mexican War brings Army of the West through Central Arizona; Kearny proclaims sovereignty of the United States in area; Cooke leads Mormon Battalion across southern Arizona, marking our army wagon road.

| 1848 | Treaty of Guadalupe Hidalgo pledges United States to pacify boundary along Gila River and Rio Grande, marking vast Mexican cession. |

AMERICAN PERIOD — 1848-1987

1848	Treaty of Guadalupe Hidalgo brings huge undeveloped area into United States.
1849	Gold seekers use Cooke's Wagon Road in rush to California diggings.
1850	Compromise Act of 1850 establishes Territory of New Mexico, which includes Arizona north of the Gila River.
1850-51	Boundary commission under John Russell Bartlett surveys new international boundary from Rio Grande to Colorado River.
1851	Fort Defiance established in northeastern corner of Arizona.
1852	Fort Yuma on California shore of Colorado protects river crossing. Captain Lorenzo Sitgreaves leads exploring expedition along 35th parallel, then to Fort Yuma. Uncle Sam, first steamboat on Colorado.
1853	Gadsden Purchase brings United States land south of Gila extending into southern New Mexico.
1853-54	Lieutenant A. W. Whipple makes railroad survey along 35th parallel.
1854	Charles D. Poston and Herman Ehrenberg arrive in Arizona, finding interesting mining prospects.
1855	Lieutenant William H. Emory surveys international boundary extended by Gadsden Purchase.
1856	Mexican garrison leaves Tucson; U.S. Dragoons arrive. American residents of Arizona petition Congress for separation from New Mexico.
1857	Fort Buchanan established in southern Arizona.
1857-58	Lieutenant Edward F. Beale surveys wagon route on 35th parallel, using camels as pack animals.
1858	Butterfield Overland Stage begins operation across Arizona.

1859	Fort Mohave established on Colorado River in northwestern Arizona.
1861	Bascom Affair inflames Chiricahua Apaches; withdrawal of troops at outbreak of Civil War encourages Indian raiding; Arizona declares itself Confederate in bid for protection.
1862	Jefferson Davis on February 14 declares Arizona a territory of the Confederate States of America. Skirmish at Picacho Pass is only significant Civil War encounter between Confederate and Union troops in Arizona; James H. Carleton leads California Column across desert, re-establishing it as United States territory; fierce battle fought at Apache Pass between Union troops and combined Apache force under Mangas Colorado and Cochise; Fort Bowie established to guard Apache Pass.
1863	On February 24 President Lincoln signs law creating Territory of Arizona; government party sworn into office at Navajo Springs late in December. Walker Party prospects for gold in mountains near Prescott. Navajos ordered confined to reservation at Bosque Redondo, New Mexico.
1864	Capital moved from Chino Valley to new town called Prescott; First Territorial Legislature meets, Sept. 26 - Dec. 10; counties of Yuma, Mohave, Yavapai and Pima created; population 4,573, not including Indians.
1866-86	Army posts and Indian reservations provide profitable market for beef.
1867	Territorial capital moved to Tucson.
1869-77	Gov. Anson P. K. Safford crusades for public school system.
1869	John Wesley Powell leads party exploring Colorado River canyons.
1871	Camp Grant Massacre horrifies nation; President Grant institutes "peace policy" in Arizona. First telegraph line in Arizona.
1872	Gen. George Crook embarks upon military conquest of northern Apaches.
1873	Northern Apaches concentrated on San Carlos Indian Reservation.

1875	First major copper production in Arizona.
1877	Rich mineralized ledges discovered at Bisbee; Ed Scheiffelin finds silver bonanza which makes Tombstone famous boom town.
	Southern Pacific railroad reaches Fort Yuma from the west; territorial prison opened on bluff beside Colorado River.
	Territorial capital returned to Prescott.
1880	Southern Pacific completes line across Arizona to New Mexico.
1881	Atlantic and Pacific (later the Santa Fe) reaches Winslow, building westward.
1882	Outbreaks from reservation; major military operations against Apaches.
1885	Legislature appropriates first funds for higher education, authorizing university and normal school.
1886	Geronimo and renegade Chiricahua Apaches captured and exiled to Florida, ending Indian wars in Arizona.
	Higher education started with opening of Arizona Territorial Normal School at Tempe.
1888	Copper replaces gold and silver in economic importance in Arizona.
1889	Capital makes final, permanent move to Phoenix.
1891	University of Arizona holds first classes.
1893	Demonetization of silver hurts Arizona mining industry.
1899	Northern Arizona Normal School at Flagstaff established.
1901	Grand Canyon connected to Santa Fe railroad by spur line.
1902	Plan for joint statehood of Arizona and New Mexico causes several years of quarreling.
1903	Salt River Valley Water Users' Association formed; becomes model for other irrigation districts in nation.
1907	Gambling prohibited in Arizona.
1910	Arizona Enabling Act passed by Congress; Constitutional Convention meets.

1911	Theodore Roosevelt dedicates completed Tonto (Roosevelt) Dam on Salt River.
	President Taft vetoes admission of Arizona in opposition to recall of judges; Arizona agrees to make the change demanded by President; first election of statehood officials.
1912	Arizona admitted to Union as 48th state on February 14; within nine months recall of judges restored to constitution.
	Plank highway built across sand dunes west of Yuma.
1917	Nation's first municipal airport established at Tucson.
	Mining boom in Arizona threatened by strike fostered by I.W.W.; Bisbee Deportation causes national stir.
1919	Grand Canyon becomes national park.
1926	First scheduled commercial air service in Arizona.
1928	Coolidge Dam completed and dedicated by President Calvin Coolidge.
1930	The planet Pluto discovered at Lowell Observatory, Flagstaff.
1936	President Franklin Delano Roosevelt dedicates Boulder Dam, later to be re-named Hoover Dam.
1941	Clouds of war bring increased military operations to Arizona.
1946	American Institute for Foreign Trade established at closed air training field near Glendale.
	Arizona right-to-work law becomes effective; industrial development and manufacturing take on new importance.
1953	Closing of United Verde Extension Mine marks end of fabulous mining span at Jerome; "ghost town" remains.
1963	Arizona wins United States Supreme Court decision in long contest for share of Colorado River water; hope revived that Central Arizona Project can be achieved.
1964	Senator Barry Goldwater, Republican Party nominee for President.

1968	Enactment of Colorado Basin Act authorized construction of Central Arizona Project.
	Senator Carl Hayden retired after representing Arizona in the House of the Senate since 1912.
1971	Jack Williams .... began serving first four year term as Governor.
1973	Vietnam .... Prisoners of war return to Arizona
1975	Raul H. Castro .... inaugurated as the first Mexican American Governor.
1977	Wesley Bolin becomes Governor of Arizona.
1978	Bruce Babbitt becomes Governor of Arizona.
1980	Senator Barry Goldwater re-elected to the United States Senate
1981	Justice Sandra O'Connor from Arizona becomes first woman appointed to U.S. Supreme Court
1982	Because of the increase of population, Arizona will add a new Congressman
1982	Palo Verde Nuclear Plant, 50 miles west of Phoenix nears completion.
	Is world's largest nuclear plant.
1985	Palo Verde Nuclear Plant begins partial operation. Will be in full operation in 1987. Largest nuclear plant in the free world.
1985	Oscar Palmer inventor and philandropist dies.
1986	Evan Mecham elected republican governor of Arizona.
1986	William H. Rehnquist of Phoenix appointed Chief Justice of the U.S. Supreme Court.
1986	Sun City Vistoso begins to be built in Tucson. It is the third active adult community to be built by Del Webb Communities, Inc.
1987	Arizona State University football team selected to represent Pac Ten in Rose Bowl, January 1, 1987. Defeats the University of Michigan, 22-15.
1987	Frank X. Gordon Jr., first person of Polish descent becomes chief justice of Arizona Supreme Court.
1987	Pope John Paul visits Phoenix.
1988	Governor Evan Mecham impeached.

CHAPTER 24.

Arizona Statistics

ARIZONA'S LAND OWNERSHIP

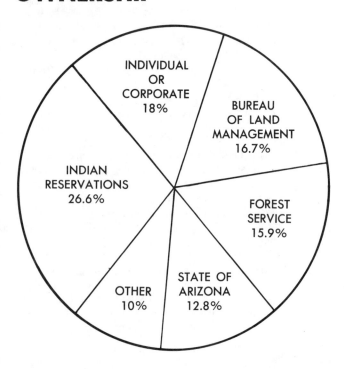

Arizona's Governors

Territorial

John N. Goodwin	1863-66	Nathan O. Murphy	1892-93
Richard C. McCormick	1866-69	Louis C. Hughes	1892-96
A. P. K. Safford	1869-77	Benjamin J. Franklin	1896-97
John P. Hoyt	1877-78	Myron H. McCord	1897-98
John C. Fremont	1878-81	Nathan O. Murphy	1898-02
Frederick Tritle	1881-85	Alexander O. Brodie	1902-05
C. Meyer Zulich	1885-89	Joseph H. Kibby	1905-09
Lewis Wolfley	1889-90	Richard E. Sloan	1909-12
John N. Irwin	1890-92		

State

George W. P. Hunt	1912-17	J. Howard Pyle	1951-55
Thomas E. Campbell	1917-17	Ernest W. McFarland	1955-59
George W. P. Hunt	1917-19	Paul Fannin	1959-65
Thomas E. Campbell	1919-23	Sam P. Goddard	1965-67
George W. P. Hunt	1923-29	John R. Williams	1967-75
John C. Phillips	1929-31	Raul Castro	1975-77
George W. P. Hunt	1931-33	Wesley Bolin	1977-78
Benjamin Moeur	1933-37	Bruce Babbitt	1978-86
R. C. Stanford	1937-39	Evan Mecham	1986-88
R. T. Jones	1939-41	Rose Mofford	1988-91
Sidney P. Osborn	1941-48	J. Fife Symington III	1991-
Dan E. Garvey	1948-51		

Members In
U.S. Congress

Senators

Henry F. Ashurst...1912-1941
Marcus A. Smith...1912-1921
Ralph H. Cameron 1921-1927
Carl Hayden..1927-1969
Ernest W. McFarland 1941-1953
Barry Goldwater 1953-1986
Paul Fannin...1965-1977
Dennis DeConcini..1977-1994
John McCain..1987-

Representatives

Carl Hayden...1912-1927
Lewis W. Douglas...1927-1933
Mrs. Isabella Greenway 1933-1937
John R. Murdock 1937-1943
Richard Harless...1943-1949
Harold A. Patten 1949-1953
Stewart Udall 1955-1960
John Rhodes...1953-1982
Morris Udall 1955-1960
George F. Senner, Jr. 1963-1967
Sam Steiger..1967-1977
John Conlan 1973-1977
Eldon Rudd 1977-1986
Robert Stump...1977-
Jim Kolbe...1985-
Jon Kyl...1986-
Jay Rhodes 1986-1992
Ed Pastor...1991-

CHAPTER 25.

Arizona, Today and Tomorrow

If I had to pick one man in the history of Arizona who contributed more to this state than any other, it would have to be Senator Carl Hayden.

Barry Goldwater in an interview
with author in 1994

Historically, Arizona has relied on her four C's as the foundation for an economic base: cattle, copper, cotton and climate. While this is still true to a certain degree, the author in this book has repeatedly pointed out how Arizona has become a manufacturing State. Its success in the future in this field will ultimately depend on her availability of energy and water.

About one half of Arizona's manufacturing employees work in advanced technology industries such as electronic components, computers, ordnance, aircraft and parts. Smelting and refining copper ore, and forest products are also significant employers. Most employment is concentrated in the Phoenix and Tucson areas with notable exceptions of smelters and forest product firms.

Arizona is and will be one of the leading states in the field of solar energy. A bright future is predicted in this important category of energy development.

People will always be moving to warmer climates for health reasons. Arizona is a haven for these people.

Arizona is a retirement community. The Senior Citizens find so many qualities in the life here that have a direct appeal to them. From the viewpoint of economics, they can live in Arizona for less money. This fact alone brings thousands to this celestial oasis. The life style is slower in the desert communities.

The political landscape will be changing in Arizona in 1994. Senator DeConcini is retiring after giving Arizona outstanding leadership for many years. As a Democrat he contributed much to his party and will be missed. Representative John Kyle, a Republican, is running for his seat in the Senate. Congressman Sam Coppersmith, a Democrat, is abandoning his seat in District One and will be a candidate for the U.S. Senate. Many are vying to replace Coppersmith in District One. Among the many, Bert Tollefson, a Republican, is expected to win. He has had a brilliant career in government, having held ambassador rank in the State Department, was the chief assistant to Ezra Benton, Secretary of Agriculture, in the Eisenhower administration for four years, and has been highly successful in the real estate business in Arizona. Governor Symington, a Republican, will seek a second term but his two rivals from the Democratic party will give him a contested battle for the seat. Eddie Basha, the supermarket magnate and Terry Goddard, the former Mayor of Phoenix, are very much in the race.

With the earthquakes, the horrible fires that hit the Malibu area, the depressing state of the economy . . . . . all hitting California at once in the months of 1993, many residents have decided to leave the state. Hence, thousands are coming to Arizona to live permanently. In a few years Arizona will have a population over 5 million. A huge boom is expected.

To challenge this growth Arizona is fortunate to have the long awaited Central Arizona Project completed. This is a 336 mile concrete lifeline bringing the much needed water from the Colorado River. It was finished in 1994. The state now has enough water to meet the needs of further growth. The federal government financed the project and now Arizona must pay this debt back over a 54 year period. Arizona has vast lands that can now be developed and a land boom which is coming, may be the biggest in this state's history. Real estate has long been a profitable market for investors in Arizona running to billions of dollars in recent years.

The Tawa Real Estate and Investment firm located at the Tawa Center, 13430 North Scottsdale Road in Scottsdale, is one of the most successful companies operating in Arizona. It is owned and operated by two brothers from Canada, Frank Chiappetta, CFO, and Tony Chiappetta, CEO, with Peter Osmundson as the designated broker. The Tawa Center is the headquarters for this well known company. They are a full service brokerage and management firm looking for more property, either on a fee or portfolio basis.